EXTRAORDINARY LOVE

Live Every Moment with God, Reflections on the First Letter of John

PIETER F. THERON

CONTENTS

Introduction	vii
1. Falling in Love with God	1
2. Contend for Your Soul	8
3. Jesus Is Real	18
4. Fellowship with God	27
5. Living the Jesus Life—Believe and Obey (Part 1)	35
6. Living the Jesus Life—Believe and Obey! (Part 2)	46
7. We Have Overcome	54
8. Love the Lord, Not the World	63
9. Remain in Christ	75
10. Sailing with Christ	84
11. Keep on Abiding in Christ	89
12. Children of God Live Right and Love Others	96
13. Believe and Love with Confidence	104
14. We are from God, We are People of Truth	115
15. God is Love, Love Lives In Us	124
16. God is Life, God Gives Life	133
17. We Know the True God. Live with Confidence.	143
18. You Can Live the Deeper Life	153
Acknowledgments	165
Bibliography	169
About the Author	173

Copyright © 2019 Pieter F. Theron
All rights reserved. No part of this publication may be reproduced, distributed, or transmitted in any form or by any means, including photocopying, recording, or other electronic or mechanical methods, without the prior written permission of the publisher, except in the case of brief quotations embodied in reviews and certain other noncommercial uses permitted by copyright law.

All Scripture quotations, unless otherwise indicated, are taken from the Holy Bible, New International Version®, NIV®. Copyright ©1973, 1978, 1984, 2011 by Biblica, Inc.™ Used by permission of Zondervan. All rights reserved worldwide. www.zondervan.comThe "NIV" and "New International Version" are trademarks registered in the United States Patent and Trademark Office by Biblica, Inc.™

ebook ISBN-13: 978-1-7332496-0-7

print ISBN-13: 978-1-7332496-1-4

To all followers of Jesus Christ who desire to experience God's extraordinary love and to love others with extraordinary love and so change the world.

INTRODUCTION

Extraordinary love is unreasonable love that cannot be explained in human terms. Extraordinary love is unconditional love that loves without expecting anything in return, undeserved love that is self-giving, loving first before being loved.

We desperately need extraordinary love. We live in a world that is filled with fear, anxiety, and hatred. There are so many divisions, conflicts, and sorrows. Life seems to be either meaningless or all about looking out for self.

Is there more to life than this? How can we overcome fear and anxiety in these times? How can we overcome hatred, divisions, and conflicts? How can we live with joy, peace, confidence, and contentment in the midst of pain and suffering?

THERE IS A WAY ...

There is a way, and it is the way of extraordinary love. It is the love for God that is expressed and lived out in love for others. It is the love that seeks the benefit and good of the other. It is love that seeks truth and beauty. It is a real, authentic, sincere love. Yes, love that even loves our enemies. Love that places others above ourselves. It is love that makes us willing to give our life for others.

We can experience and give this extraordinary love by falling in love with God more and more. As we experience God's love and love God, we learn to love others. As we experience God's love, we learn to live the deeper spiritual life. We learn to live every moment with God, experiencing love, joy, peace, confidence, courage, and contentment.

Our treasure, our passion, our life's desire is where our hearts are. When our hearts are filled with God's love and love for him, we begin to care for what he cares for. We begin to see people, things, and the world through his eyes. As we live every moment with God, as we grow into a deeper relationship with him, our love for him, for others, and for the world increases and drives us to live with vision, purpose, and passion.

The deeper life is about God's extraordinary love transforming us to love others with extraordinary love.

This book is about falling in love with God, experiencing his extraordinary love, and allowing his love to change us.

Changed Lives

God blessed me to live and serve for many years in different countries and cultures. I have seen how people's lives have changed when they discovered the love of God and fell in love with him; or when they rediscovered God's love, remembering their first love for him.

I have seen cynical and skeptical people regain their vision. I have seen people who have given up on the world and society renew their mission to work for change and the betterment of others. I have seen people who have given up on life burn again with passion, living with renewed purpose.

Many people have been disappointed and given up on the church. Some even gave up on their faith. Rediscovering God's love and their love for God restored and healed them. They

INTRODUCTION

recommitted themselves to serve others, build God's kingdom, and live for God's glory.

I know a man very well who followed Jesus with passion. He committed his life to full-time service for God. And then his passion dried up. He lost vision. He was disappointed in God—that God was not fulfilling his part of the bargain they entered into when he accepted the call. He wanted to live his own life, pursue his own dreams, get out of the ministry game—do his own thing. But then God intervened (in many ways), and this man decided to give God another chance. He learned to die to himself. He gave everything up, surrendering everything to God and trusting him anew.

Something extraordinary happened to this man. His first love for God was rekindled, and since that time that love-fire has burned with increasing intensity. His life was re-centered and refocused on God. Out of that renewed, intimate love relationship with God flowed love for others. A vision, mission, and passion were born to live for others and to help others experience this deeper life with God, the Jesus-life of love.

Yes, you guessed right. That man is me. But this book is not about me, or my story. This book is about how God pursues us and how our experience of his extraordinary love changes us. It is about what happens when we start to really abide in Jesus Christ. I have been blessed to experience that extraordinary love and hope that you will also experience God's extraordinary love through this book.

FALLING IN LOVE WITH GOD AND OTHERS

This book is adapted from a series of teachings that I taught in our church. These teachings were based on and walked us through the first letter of John in the New Testament. The first two chapters introduce the series giving an overview and explaining the deeper life. The next chapters walk us through

INTRODUCTION

First John passage by passage, and the last chapter concludes the series by bringing it all together.

My vision and prayer for this book are that it will show you how to contend for your soul by pursuing a deeper relationship with God. I want to take you out of your comfort zone. I want you to become discontent with your spiritual life. If you are experiencing and living the deeper life, good, but I want you to know that there is more. I want you to go even further. If you have become complacent, I want you to wake up and pursue God. And if you have not yet experienced the deeper life with God, I hope that you will encounter him through Jesus Christ, and begin to abide in Christ.

Falling in love with God will impact your daily life and all areas of your life—your family, your work, your finances, your friends, your leadership, your play, and your recreation. Falling in love with God will result in falling in love with others. It will mean you work with a passion for their good.

Your life will be transformed. You will have a new vision and purpose. You will live and work with renewed passion. This extraordinary love will flow out of you. It will impact and change others around you. It will change society and the world, even if only in small ways, but those changes will make the Kingdom of God real and visible in this world. It will help others to experience God's extraordinary love.

JOIN THIS ADVENTURE OF EXTRAORDINARY LOVE

To experience this extraordinary love, you must step out of your comfort zone and complacency. Open yourself. Be willing to be changed. Be willing to give yourself up. Allow God to meet you, to work in you, to transform you.

Do not just read *this* book. Also, read the first letter of John

INTRODUCTION

and the other Scriptures referred to in the book. Study and meditate on the passage from John that each chapter explores.

Take action. Reflect on what you have learned in each chapter. I have included reflection questions and action steps at the end of most of the chapters. Stop, pause, reflect on these, answer them, and allow the Word of God to penetrate your soul and sink deep into your heart.

Utilize the practical action steps within each chapter. A deeper life with God does not happen by itself or automatically. You must contend for your soul. It is an act of the will, an intentional decision to step out, take action, and pursue God as he has pursued you.

If you want to finish a long-distance race you must practice every day. There are certain disciplines, skills, and practices you need to do every day to prepare for the race. This takes self-discipline and will enable you to run the race, to persevere, to enjoy yourself, and to finish.

The same principle applies to the deeper life. Take action, practice the spiritual disciplines every day, abide in Christ, and you will begin to live the deeper spiritual life. You will learn to live every moment with God with love, peace, joy, confidence, and contentment. You will run the race and finish it well! And at the finish line, your Lord will wait for you, and say, "Well done, good and faithful servant!"

1

FALLING IN LOVE WITH GOD

FOR SOME TIME, the Holy Spirit has laid it on my heart to teach about the deeper life or the deeper walk with God as some would call it. I avoided and postponed this for a long time. So many have written about the deeper life. What could I add that is new or different? What do I really know about the deeper life?

However, my heart's desire to follow after God, to live the deeper life, and the insistence of the Holy Spirit brought me back to this again and again until I could no longer avoid it. Finally, I gave in and taught this sermon series that evolved into this book. I learned and grew much with our church as we explored, read, studied God's Word, and reflected together on the deeper life.

So here is the book based on the sermon series.

How do we follow Jesus in today's culture? A culture that questions everything Jesus stands for. A culture that exerts pressure and entices us to not follow Jesus, but to live in and walk in the ways of the world?

Spirituality—the spiritual life—has everything to do with living the practical Christian life. Living the Christian life is not about recipes, projects, or meetings. The deeper life is not a self-improvement or a self-help regimen. It is not only about what you are doing, but also about who you are and who you are becoming.[1] How you live and what you do flow out of who you are.

Jesus said, "A good man brings good things out of the good stored up in his heart, and an evil man brings evil things out of the evil stored up in his heart. For the mouth speaks what the heart is full of." (Luke 6:45)

In Matthew 15:18-19, he said, "But the things that come out of a person's mouth come from the heart, and these defile them. For out of the heart come evil thoughts—murder, adultery, sexual immorality, theft, false testimony, slander."

Jesus also tells us, "For where your treasure is, there your heart will be also." (Matt. 6:21)

What is our treasure? Where are our hearts? What have we stored up in our hearts?

Who we are and what we do flow out of the soul and heart. When the heart does not belong to God, when the soul is broken or lost, it is impossible or extremely difficult to live the Christian life. It leads to hypocritical, two-faced, and self-centered living. We believe one thing, we say one thing, but our actions, deeds, and lives show something different.

Why do our souls matter?

The well-being of our soul is of the utmost importance. The deeper life is about taking care of our souls, making sure that our hearts belong to God. Heart transformation comes before behavior modification. In other words, before we can change our behavior, our actions, and our lives, we must first change our hearts and make sure they are in the right place. For revival to happen in the lives of Jesus followers, for revival to happen in the church, in our country, and in the world, we must return to our first love—God. (Rev. 2:4)

> *One of the teachers of the law came and heard them debating. Noticing that Jesus had given them a good answer, he asked him, "Of all the commandments, which is the most important?"*

"The most important one," answered Jesus, "is this: 'Hear, O Israel: The Lord our God, the Lord is one. Love the Lord your God with all your heart and with all your soul and with all your mind and with all your strength.' The second is this: 'Love your neighbor as yourself.' There is no commandment greater than these."

"Well said, teacher," the man replied. "You are right in saying that God is one and there is no other but him. To love him with all your heart, with all your understanding and with all your strength, and to love your neighbor as yourself is more important than all burnt offerings and sacrifices."

When Jesus saw that he had answered wisely, he said to him, "You are not far from the kingdom of God." And from then on, no one dared ask him any more questions. (Mark 12:28-34)

1. What is the Deeper Life?

A.W. Tozer said, "The deeper spiritual life is not something just to be talked about—it is a quiet enjoyment of daily blessing, peace, and victory that is lived day by day beyond empty profession and without any two-faced circumstances!"[2]

John Ortberg, using the words of Dallas Willard, describes it as the total contentment, joy, and confidence in your everyday experience and living with God.[3] It is the inexpressible and glorious joy that Peter speaks of in 1 Peter 1:8-9, "Though you have not seen him, you love him; and even though you do not see him now, you believe in him and are filled with an inexpressible and glorious joy, for you are receiving the end result of your faith, the salvation of your souls."[4]

The deeper life is living the new, eternal life here, now and forever. To quote John Ortberg again, "The salvation of your soul is not just about where you go when you die. The word salvation means healing or deliverance at the deepest level of who we are in the care of God through the presence of Jesus."[5]

What is eternal life?

Jesus answered, "Now this is eternal life: that they know you, the only true God, and Jesus Christ, whom you have sent." (John 17:3) The Hebrew and Greek words used for "know"[6] in the Old and New Testament speaks of a deep, intimate knowledge that comes from experiencing God in a very close, intimate relationship. It is not just head knowledge, but knowing with your whole being—body and soul—because you are experiencing God intimately.

Eternal life is about the quality of life with God, not just the duration of life into eternity.[7] Eternal life is the with-God-life, living in God's presence, here in this life as well as in the eternities. It is to know God, delight in God, and to love God more than we know, delight in, or love anything else.[8]

Jesus Christ made and makes the deeper life possible. His death and resurrection made the new, deeper life real. And when we abide in Christ, the deeper life becomes real. We know and experience God in Jesus Christ. Because Jesus is the Son of God, Jesus *is* God. When we abide in Christ, we are living the Jesus way of life with God.

The deeper life is possible when we live in the power of the Holy Spirit. The more we submit our hearts to the Holy Spirit, the deeper our life with God will become. Thus, the deeper life is a God-focused, Christ-centered, Spirit-filled life.

What matters is not the accomplishments we achieve, nor a life of empty religious activities.[9] What matters is the person we are becoming in Christ through the power of the Holy Spirit. What matters most, is that we love God above all else, and with our whole being.

But this is not all the deeper life is about. Listen to what the Great Commandment of love says. "Love your neighbor as yourself." Our love for God is expressed, shown, made real, concrete, and practical through loving others. The deeper life is a life of loving others—loving our brothers and sisters in Christ, loving unbelievers and sinners, loving even our enemies.

Loving God and others will translate into a life of making disciples of others. When you have experienced God's love and the unspeakable joy of the new, eternal life, you will want to share this with others. When you love people, you will want them to experience the deeper life.

Loving people is seeing them through God's eyes. The love of Christ compels us to make disciples of all peoples.

> *Then Jesus came to them and said, "All authority in heaven and on earth has been given to me. Therefore go and make disciples of all nations, baptizing them in the name of the Father and of the Son and of the Holy Spirit, and teaching them to obey everything I have commanded you. And surely I am with you always, to the very end of the age." (Matt. 28:18-20)*

2. Why the Deeper Life?

Why is the deeper life so important? Once you have tasted its unspeakable joy you will want more. And of course, the well-being of our soul is of the utmost importance. We must take care of our souls and contend for our souls as we will see in the next chapter. But, this is not only about the salvation of our own souls. The deeper life is not just about ourselves. There is a bigger picture. The deeper life is about God's glory, about God's kingdom, his purpose, and his mission.

Our Lord Jesus Christ gave us these two great commandments, the Great Commandment to love and the Great Commission to make disciples. I see these two commandments as the pillars of the deeper life.

First, we are called to know and love God, to worship and glorify him in everything we do. Then we are called to make God known to others who will also love him, worship, and glorify him.

Everything culminates in love—God's love for us and for the world, and our love for God and our fellow human beings. The deeper life in Jesus Christ through the power of the Holy Spirit enables us to be a community and a church that loves. A people that love God above everything else, and that love other people as ourselves. This love compels, motivates, and mobilizes us to share the good news of salvation with others and to make disciples of others, no matter what the cost.

But, we can only become and make disciples when we are transformed into the image of Christ, living and cultivating the deeper life. Jesus is calling out to us, "Come to Me; become Mine; become like Me; follow Me into the lives of those for whom I died."[10] In our world, many Christians' and churches' commitment to their faith runs only skin-deep. The world desperately needs authentic followers of Jesus.

How can Jesus be present in the world?

Through each of us personally, and through the church corporately. Thomas Ashbrook says, "It is fundamentally who we are, rather than what we do, that makes us authentic children of God, the Body of Christ, the church. We can give away only what we have received. We can proclaim only what we are authentically living."[11] He goes on to say that the Holy Trinity is present in us "and in the world, moving forward mightily in His plan to save His beloved people. God is dwelling in the mansions of your heart, calling you into the deepest intimacy and joy in His love. He is calling you to know Him so completely that you will burn with His love for you and for the world. He is calling us to fully join Him in the adventure of the Kingdom of God."[12]

Isn't that exciting? Don't you want to be a part of that? We need a revival. We need to return to our first love, God, and to live the deeper life for the sake of God's kingdom and his glory.

REFLECTION

1. What does the deeper life mean for you?

ACTION

1. Make some time to read through First John. Use the

version that you are used to and most comfortable with. Read through the whole letter in one sitting. This is not a Bible study. Just read through the whole book slowly, attentively.

2. Take note of the time it took to read through the whole book. Now plan to read through First John once every day for the next thirty days. You can use your personal devotions for this or set aside special time if possible.

---

1. See Dallas Willard quoted by John Ortberg, "The most important thing in your life ... is not what you do; it's who you become" in John Ortberg, *Soul Keeping: Caring For the Most Important Part of You* (Grand Rapids, MI: Zondervan, 2014), 23, Kindle.
2. A.W. Tozer, "Tozer Devotional: Beyond Empty Profession, Tue, November 03, 2015," The Alliance Tozer Devotional, accessed December 12, 2018, https://www.cmalliance.org/devotions/tozer?id=253.
3. Ortberg, *Soul Keeping*, 89,90,98, Kindle.
4. Ortberg, 48, Kindle.
5. Ortberg, 48, Kindle.
6. Greek — γινώσκω (ginóskō); Hebrew — יָדַע (yā·ḏă').
7. Ortberg, 118, Kindle.
8. This statement is derived from the idea expressed by John Piper, "Training the next generation of Evangelical pastors and missionaries," (plenary address delivered at the annual meeting and fiftieth anniversary of the Evangelical Theological Society, Orlando, Florida, November 20, 1998, accessed December 12, 2019, https://www.desiringgod.org/messages/training-the-next-generation-of-evangelical-pastors-and-missionaries.
9. See Ortberg, 121, Kindle.
10. R. Thomas Ashbrook, *Mansions of the Heart: Exploring the Seven Stages of Spiritual Growth*, (San Francisco, CA: Jossey-Bass, 2009), Kindle loc. 4634-4635.
11. Ashbrook, *Mansions*, Kindle loc. 4646-4648.
12. Ashbrook, Kindle loc. 4686-4689.

2
CONTEND FOR YOUR SOUL

WHAT DO you want for your life? Why are you here in this place at this time? Is there more to life than this? Where are you heading to? What do you hunger for? What do you want in your walk with God? Consider a few situations. They may or may not ring true for you in your life.

You go to church every Sunday and are involved in church ministries. But you are tired, perhaps even cynical. You have been hearing for years how abundant and full life in Christ is supposed to be, but inside you feel dry and empty. You may even enjoy Sunday worship. You walk out and think, "That was a good sermon, good music, great fellowship. But now let's get back to real life."[1]

Or you want to change, to live the Christian life. This is what we call white-knuckle change. By sheer will and determination, you try to change your life. You do your devotions, read your Bible, pray on your knees. Then you get up with firm resolutions: "Today, I will live a holy life. I will practice love, joy, peace and patience today." But five minutes later, on your way to work, a driver cuts in front of you. And you shout at him in anger.

Some people want to follow Jesus or are following Jesus, but they reject the church because they don't want to be like the

Christians who claim to believe in love, forgiveness, and new life, but instead live in fear, judgment, selfishness, and pettiness. They do this, not realizing that with this attitude, they have already become like those they reject: judgmental, self-righteous, self-centered, and guilty of spiritual pride.

Wilbourne in his book, *Union with Christ*, tells of a skeptical friend who asked him, "If the gospel is supernatural, as you say, then why doesn't it seem to make more of a difference in the lives of so many who claim to believe it?"[2]

1. Mind the Gap[3]

There is a gap between what we Christians claim is true about ourselves, and what we often see when we look at ourselves in the mirror. Yes, I say look at "ourselves." It is so easy to see that gap in others' lives, but do we see the gap in our own lives? The problem is this: How do we integrate our faith in our everyday lives? How do we connect God with our daily lives?[4]

There is a gap. The first step toward the deeper life is to recognize this gap and admit its existence in our lives. We must mind the gap. If we don't mind it, we may fall into the gap, walk in darkness, and never experience the deeper life.

However, some things may prevent us from minding the gap. I borrowed these examples from Wilbourne's book.[5]

- "If you never try to connect the truths of God to your everyday life;" if you build walls between the "sacred" life of the church and the secular, real world out there, then you will not notice this gap.
- If you keep Jesus and his authority, his Lordship, safely tucked away in heaven where he cannot influence or threaten your way of going about life, then you will not be concerned about this gap.
- "If you believe that the gospel means you have a ticket to heaven when you die," and that God's "grace means

you don't need to strive to obey Jesus Christ while you live" in this world;
- "If you believe Jesus' words, 'It is finished' means there's nothing left for you to do," and
- "If you consider Jesus' call to discipleship to be optional, reserved for" the super-committed, the super-spiritual ones—then you will not see this gap. And sadly, many Christians have lived with this gap for so long, that they have become used to it, and they no longer mind it.[6]

To mind and overcome this gap, to experience God every moment, to live the deeper life, we must contend for our souls.[7]

2. What is the Soul?[8]

But what is the soul? And here I tremble with fear because in trying to answer this question we are walking on holy ground and dealing with one of God's great mysteries. It is not the purpose of this chapter to answer this question fully. I want to focus on our calling to contend for our souls. I give only a very brief explanation to help us understand why our souls are so important.

Human beings consist of different elements, or "parts," that make up a human life and the whole person.

- We have bodies—our face, appearance, and actions.
- We have a will—our intentions—with which we choose.
- We have a mind—our thoughts, feelings, values, and conscience.
- We are social beings created to live in relationships with others.
- And then we are souls. The soul integrates our will,

mind, body and relationships into one life, into an integral, whole person.[9]

We are souls.

Genesis 2:7 says, "Then the Lord God formed a man from the dust of the ground and breathed into his nostrils the breath of life, and the man became a living being." The Hebrew word used for being, *nefesh*, is also used for soul. So it can also read, "and the man became a living soul."

We are souls "made by God, made for God, and made to need God, which means [we] were not made to be self-sufficient."[10] We were made to live in God's presence, connected to God. Who are we? Willard says it like this: "You are an unceasing spiritual being with an eternal destiny in God's great universe."[11] When our souls are connected to God we have healthy souls, and we experience the deeper life with God.

But something is broken in our souls. In the beginning, God created the perfect home for our souls: a garden of perfection where he could be with us,[12] and we with him. But we made a choice. We rejected God because we wanted to be like God. We wanted to be our own gods. We removed ourselves from God. And so death came because of sin. Our souls are lost because we are disconnected from the Source of Life. Apart from God, there is no life for our souls. We alone cannot fix, heal, or save our souls.

Only Jesus can save our souls, heal our souls, and restore our soul's connection with God. God did not give up on us. In his amazing love and grace, God pursues us relentlessly. He sent his Son, Jesus Christ, who died for us, and was resurrected so that we can have new, eternal life. Jesus is the Life. In Jesus, we can again enter into, live in, and experience the presence of God. Our souls can live again, now and forever.

3. Contend for Your Soul![13]

So now, we are saved. We can now say, "Jesus is my Lord and Savior. I am in Christ, and Christ is in me. I have a new, eternal life." But we must also ask, "How do I live this new life? How do I mind the gap? How can I experience the deeper life?"

We must contend for our souls!

Paul says this in Philippians 2:12-16:

> *Therefore, my dear friends, as you have always obeyed—not only in my presence but now much more in my absence—continue to work out your salvation with fear and trembling, for it is God who works in you to will and to act in order to fulfill his good purpose. Do everything without grumbling or arguing, so that you may become blameless and pure, "children of God without fault in a warped and crooked generation." Then you will shine among them like stars in the sky as you hold firmly to the word of life. And then I will be able to boast on the day of Christ that I did not run or labor in vain.*

Live the New Life We Have Received

"Work out your salvation with fear and trembling." Paul does not say that we must work to achieve our salvation. We are saved only by grace through faith. However, we are called to live the new life we have received. We are called to put into practice the salvation we have received through faith in Jesus Christ. That is what it means to contend for our souls.

Why Must We Contend for Our Souls?

Because Satan is trying to destroy our souls. "Be alert and of sober mind. Your enemy the devil prowls around like a roaring lion looking for someone to devour. Resist him, standing firm in the faith ..." (1 Pet 5:8-9a)

If we do not contend for our souls, we will become susceptible to temptations and deceptions, and it will become easier to give in to these. We fall into sin or remain in sin. We become disobedient to the Lord. We come under God's judgment and wrath and are in grave danger of losing our souls. Jesus warned us, "Do not be afraid of those who kill the body but cannot kill the soul. Rather, be afraid of the One who can destroy both soul and body in hell." (Matt. 10:28)

If we do not contend for our souls, we may not be able to stand and be strong in the Lord. When things fall apart, when the going gets tough, when we are persecuted, what will we do? Will we abandon the faith and denounce our Lord?

How do we contend for our souls?

We Live the New Life through Obedience

When we obey everything that our Lord commanded and taught us, we are living the new life we have in him. What did our Lord command and teach us? What does this new life, the Jesus-life look like? Jesus describes the new life in the Sermon on the Mount in Matthew chapters five to seven. He ends his teaching with these words, "Not everyone who says to me, 'Lord, Lord,' will enter the kingdom of heaven, but only the one who does the will of my Father who is in heaven" (Matt. 7:21). And in verse 24, "Therefore everyone who hears these words of mine and puts them into practice is like a wise man who built his house on the rock." (Matt. 7:24)

We Live the New Life through Humility

We contend for our souls with fear and trembling because the living, holy, all-powerful God is working in our lives. We do so with fear and trembling because God is "the One who can destroy both soul and body" (Matt. 10:28). "It is a dreadful thing to fall into the hands of the living God." (Heb. 10:31)

Jesus paid a terrible price to save our souls and give us this new life. If we do not contend for our souls, if we do not live the new life, then we make light of what Jesus has done. He died to save our souls. He was resurrected to give us new life. Jesus is our Lord and Savior. But are we allowing him to be the Lord of our lives through obedience? Do we in humility and submission give complete control of our lives to the Lord?

We Live the New Life in the Power of the Holy Spirit

When we believe and accept Jesus Christ as Lord and Savior, the Holy Spirit fills us and gives us this new life. The Holy Spirit enables us to live the new life. We contend for our souls through the power of the Holy Spirit. But the Holy Spirit empowers and changes us only if we submit to him. We contend for our souls by walking in step with the Spirit. Later in this book, we will learn more on how to yield to and live in the power of the Spirit.

We Are Called to Action

Have nothing to do with godless myths and old wives' tales; rather, **train yourself to be godly**. *For physical training is of some value, but godliness has value for all things, holding promise for both the present life and the life to come. This is a trustworthy saying that deserves full acceptance. That is why we* **labor and strive**, *because we have put our hope in the living God, who is the Savior of all people, and especially of those who believe. Command and teach these things. Don't let anyone look down on you because you are young, but* **set an example** *for the believers in speech, in conduct, in love, in faith and in purity. Until I come,* **devote yourself** *to the public reading of Scripture, to preaching and to teaching.* **Do not neglect** *your gift, which was given you through prophecy when the body of elders laid their hands on you.* **Be diligent** *in these matters;* **give yourself wholly** *to them, so that everyone may see your progress.* **Watch your life and doctrine**

***closely**. **Persevere** in them, because if you do, you will save both yourself and your hearers. (Emphasis added--1 Timothy 4:7-16)*

Train yourself to be godly; labor and strive; set an example; devote yourself; be diligent; give yourself wholly. Watch your life and doctrine closely. Persevere in them, because if you do, you will save both yourself and your hearers.

We are called to action. There are many other biblical passages that talk about contending for our souls.[14] These say guard your heart, press on, run the race, flee from all this, pursue righteousness, godliness, faith, love endurance and gentleness, fight the good fight, throw off everything that hinders and the sin that so easily entangles, take hold of the eternal life to which you were called and be strong in the Lord. These are all action words calling us to action.

CONTEND FOR THE SOULS OF OTHERS

Contending for our souls is also contending for the souls of others. We have experienced the extraordinary love of Christ and the unspeakable joy of new life through Christ. This love of Christ in us compels us (2 Cor. 5:14) to share the good news of this new life with others. It compels us to contend for the souls of others. Paul told the elders in Acts 20, "Keep watch over yourselves and all the flock." I believe that this applies to all believers because we are all part of the one body of Christ. As members of the one body, we love, care for, serve, and encourage one another. We especially encourage one another to contend for our souls.

RELY ON THE LORD, NOT ON YOURSELF

If we do not contend for our souls, we will run out of steam. We will become self-reliant, relying on our own human powers, skills and abilities. We will end up doing God's work through human means.

For example, as a preacher, I sometimes fall into a trap. I rely on my skills of interpreting the Bible, my knowledge of Greek and Hebrew, and my performance as a communicator to prepare and deliver a sermon. I do not pray and listen enough to the Holy Spirit's teaching. I do not trust the power of God's living Word. Or, as a missionary, I rely on all kinds of missions methods, techniques, and strategies to make converts, plant churches, and increase the number of church attendees. I do not seek God's will in these approaches. I do not trust that this is God's work and that he will accomplish his purposes. I burn myself out thinking that it all depends on me. And when we hit that big pothole along our journey, we will not have a deep well of spiritual resources to draw from. That big pothole might just trip us up, get us under, and destroy us.[15]

BE STRONG IN THE LORD, PUT ON THE FULL ARMOR OF GOD

We contend for our souls by putting on the full armor of God through prayer. We must be strong in the Lord.

All this talk of action might tempt us into activism and busyness when what we actually need is to nurture our souls through the power of stillness, by abiding in Christ. Even though we are called to contend for our souls, we cannot do this on our own and in our own power. Jesus calls us to remain in him, and he will remain in us. Apart from him, we can do nothing (John 15:5). That is why Paul says, "I strenuously contend with all the energy Christ so powerfully works in me" (Col. 1:28) and why Hebrews 12 says that we must run this race with our eyes fixed on Jesus. Remain in Jesus, abide in Christ. This is the action we must take. This is how we contend for our souls.

We must make sure that our souls stay connected to God. It is only there, in the presence of God the Father, through Jesus

Christ and by the power of the Holy Spirit that our souls are restored, healed, and saved. Then we will live the deeper life: We will mind the gap, bridge the gap, and live with and experience God every moment of our lives, loving God and others.

REFLECTION

1. What is your understanding of contending for your soul?
2. How have you been contending for your soul?

---

1. See Rankin Wilbourne, *Union with Christ: The Way to Know and Enjoy God* (Colorado Springs, CO: David C Cook, 2016), Kindle loc 321-324.
2. Wilbourne, *Union*, Kindle loc 313-314.
3. This idea of the gap and minding the gap is based on and adopted from Wilbourne, *Union*. See chapter 1 of his book, and especially Kindle loc. 311.
4. See Wilbourne, Kindle loc 321-324.
5. Wilbourne, Kindle loc, 321-327.
6. Wilbourne, Kindle loc, 321-327.
7. Credit for the concept of contending for our souls must go to Randy Shaw, "Contend for Your Soul," teaching delivered at the annual Field Forum of the Alliance Northwest Field, Portland, OR, April 24, 2017, my personal notes taken during the teaching.
8. For this section and the explanation of the soul I am indebted to John Ortberg and Dallas Willard as quoted and referred to by Ortberg. See John Ortberg, *Soul Keeping: Caring For the Most Important Part of You* (Grand Rapids, MI: Zondervan, 2014), ch.2, 37-48, Kindle.
9. Ortberg, *Soul Keeping,* 42-43, Kindle.
10. Dallas Willard quoted by Ortberg, 39, Kindle.
11. Willard quoted by Ortberg, 111, Kindle.
12. Ortberg, 125, Kindle.
13. This section based upon and uses the ideas expressed by Shaw, "Contend for Your Soul," personal notes.
14. Read Prov 4:23; Acts 20:27-31; Col 1:28-2:1, 4:12; Phil 3:12-14, 4:8-9; 1 Cor 9:24-27; 2 Cor 10:5; Gal 5:7-10; 1 Tim 6:11-15; Heb 12:1-3.
15. See Shaw, "Contend," personal notes.

3
JESUS IS REAL

"That which was from the beginning, which we have heard, which we have seen with our eyes, which we have looked at and our hands have touched—this we proclaim concerning the Word of life. The life appeared; we have seen it and testify to it, and we proclaim to you the eternal life, which was with the Father and has appeared to us. We proclaim to you what we have seen and heard, so that you also may have fellowship with us. And our fellowship is with the Father and with his Son, Jesus Christ. We write this to make our joy complete." (1 John 1:1-4)

AS WE TALK about the deeper life, there may be several questions. Why is the deeper life important? Is it worthwhile? Is the average Christian life not enough? The deeper life sounds like a lot of hard work. It seems to be very difficult. Is it even possible? How will we know that we are living the deeper Christian life? First John helps us to understand what the deeper life is, how to live it, and how we will know that we are living it.

Before we begin to explore these questions we will first look briefly at the history and cultural context of First John. This will help us to understand John's teachings.

First John was written by John the Apostle between 85-90

A.D. He most likely wrote it in Ephesus where he lived and served in his later years before he was banned to the island of Patmos. This is actually not a letter as it does not have the usual elements of a letter. It is more a sermon, an essay, or a circular that was sent out to the church in Ephesus and Asia-Minor.[1] But since it is usually seen as a letter, we will talk about John's letter in this book.

When my wife read through First John, she said to me, "He is talking in circles." And he is. John uses a special kind of rhetoric, or logic, called spiral reasoning.[2] His thoughts are not presented in a linear way like Paul's arguments. Rather, John presents certain key themes, then comes back to them, and then repeats them again and again. But as he does this, he amplifies, expands, and goes deeper with each theme. He speaks hyperbolically, and in strong black and white terms. You could say that the volume is turned on high in First John, as he speaks strongly. John wants to make sure that his hearers get the message loud and clear.

1. The Deeper Life is All About Jesus Christ

John begins his letter with the foundation of the Christian faith: the truth about the person and work of Jesus Christ. Everything else flows out of and is based on this foundation. If we get this wrong, then everything else falls apart, and we are tempted by, and fall into, all kinds of false teachings, as well as wrong-living.

The deeper life is possible only in Jesus Christ. It is living the new life that Jesus gives us. It is living for Jesus. The deeper life is all about Jesus. The deeper life is important because it is living out the truth about what Jesus has done for us and who he is.

Jesus is fully God and fully human. It is only as God that he could be holy and righteous enough to be the atoning sacrifice for us. It is only as a human that he could die in our place. He was resurrected, ascended to heaven, was glorified, and is now ruling as the Lord. He will return to restore fully his kingdom.

If Jesus was not human and did not die, there is no atoning sacrifice for our sins. If Jesus was just a man, and was not resurrected, we have no new, eternal life, and there will be no deeper life to live.

And if he is not the ruling and coming King, we have no hope.

If this foundation is wrong or false, then we have been living in a fool's paradise for 2,000 years.

But it is true. Jesus is the Christ, the Son of God. He is God. He is the Lord and Savior of the world. And so, John begins his letter to show us that Jesus is real. He is the Truth and the Life:

> *"That which was from the beginning, which we have heard, which we have seen with our eyes, which we have looked at and our hands have touched—this we proclaim concerning the Word of life. The life appeared; we have seen it and testify to it, and we proclaim to you the eternal life, which was with the Father and has appeared to us. We proclaim to you what we have seen and heard, so that you also may have fellowship with us. And our fellowship is with the Father and with his Son, Jesus Christ. We write this to make our joy complete."* (1 John 1:1-4)

John needed to emphasize this foundation of the deeper life because he wrote to a church that was in crisis.[3] They were confronted with false teachers proclaiming all kinds of false teachings. There were divisions in the fellowship. They even experienced a church split as we see from 1 John 2:19—"They went out from us, but they did not really belong to us. For if they had belonged to us, they would have remained with us; but their going showed that none of them belonged to us."

These false teachers denied Jesus' atoning sacrifice. They asserted that he was God and not human. Therefore, he could not have died on the cross.

John's answer—Jesus was the true sacrifice for sins because he is God who became human. Only as a human could he have died as a substitute for us. Jesus is fully God and fully human.

The false teachers minimized the seriousness of sin. They claimed to have special knowledge of God and that they were without sin. They taught that it is possible to have fellowship with God, regardless of your behavior. You can live as you want, and still, have a relationship with God. They completely separated the spiritual life from the physical life. John countered and taught that our relationship with God has serious ethical implications for how we live the Christian life.

These false teachers were filled with spiritual pride and self-righteousness. They claimed to know it all and did not love others. John taught that love for others is the demonstration of, and the fruit of, genuine belief, of a relationship with God, of the Christian life, and following Jesus.

So, this was a church in serious crisis, a hurting church with many questions. This must have caused the believers to wonder: "Is the gospel true? Is what we believe true? Is Jesus real? Is Jesus the Messiah, the Savior? Is he God? Was he really human? How do we know that our faith is genuine? How do we know that we are followers of Jesus? How do we know that we are in Christ? Are we still on the right track?"

Does this sound familiar?

Today the Church, the Christian faith, is in a serious crisis. There are many false teachings going around, both inside and outside of the church. The false teachers of John's time struggled to accept that God could become human, whereas today's false teachers have difficulty believing and accepting that Jesus is God, the Son of God. He was just a man, a good teacher with great sayings, who then died. They deny his resurrection, and that he is alive today.

Evil and sin are minimized and cheap grace is taught in many churches: "We are just weak, human beings. It's natural to sin. Just confess, and God will forgive you." Although true, there seems to be little teaching on the obedience that our Lord demands, on living holy and godly lives, on contending for our souls, and on working out our salvation in fear and trembling.

There are many divisions in the Church. And if that is not enough, the Christian faith is being attacked from all sides. The Bible and biblical truth are questioned, even rejected.

The Christian rock band, Newsboys, sings about the new reality we are living in: "When did it become breaking a rule to say your name out loud in school . . . When did it become incorrect to speak the truth about life and death . . . If serving you's against the law of man, If living out my faith in you is banned . . . If saying, 'I believe' is out of line, If I'm judged 'cause I'm gonna give my life To show the world the love that fills me Then I wanna be guilty . . . Guilty of being a voice proclaiming Your ways, your truth, your life."[4]

Evil seems to be taking over. Our society is bitterly divided. And sadly, the divisions in our cultures and societies are being carried over into churches. We, who are supposed to be one, are divided, running after political and worldly views, forgetting our first love, our first allegiance and our first loyalty, Jesus Christ.

John wrote to these churches to encourage the believers, to reassure them of the truth of the gospel of Jesus Christ, and that they will have eternal life. He gives us tests or criteria by which we can know that our faith is genuine, that we are in Christ, and living the Christian life. He encourages us to grow in love of God and for one another. He encourages us to pursue the deeper life in Christ.

But if Jesus is the foundation and the focus of the deeper life, how do we know Jesus is real?

John says, "We proclaim to you what we have seen and heard" (1 John 1:3). What had John and the disciples seen and heard? "That which was from the beginning, which we have heard, which we have seen with our eyes, which we have looked at and our hands have touched" (1 John 1:1). They had seen the life, the eternal life, which was revealed to them. They had empirical evidence for what they were proclaiming.

First, Jesus is God. He is the Word. He is the life. He is eternal life. He was from the beginning, and He was with the Father. These verses remind us of Genesis 1:1 and the gospel of John, chapter 1, verses 1-4.

Genesis 1:1—"In the beginning God created the heavens and the earth."

John 1:1-4—"In the beginning was the Word, and the Word was with God, and the Word was God. He was with God in the beginning. Through him all things were made; without him, nothing was made that has been made. In him was life, and that life was the light of all mankind."

Jesus the Word was God, through him all things were made, and in him is life.

Second, Jesus is fully human. The first disciples heard him. They heard the word of *Life*, the gospel message of salvation, from the *Word* of life who is the Truth and the Life himself. They saw him with their eyes. He was real. They looked at him. The word used here means to observe, to be a spectator of. It means to observe with intensity, admiration, and astonishment. It implies to look thoroughly at something with reflection and thinking on it, with the aim of understanding.[5] Jesus was real. They touched him with their hands.[6] Jesus was no phantom or ghost, not before his death, nor after his resurrection. He had flesh and bones. Jesus was real. Jesus is real, and he makes the deeper life possible.

2. We Live the Deeper Life in Fellowship with God

How do we live the deeper life? Is it possible? How will we know we live the deeper life?

Three times John says, "We proclaim."

What is the purpose of this proclamation? "So that you also

may have fellowship with us. And indeed our fellowship is with the Father and with his Son, Jesus Christ. We write this to make our joy complete." (1 John 1:3-4)

Because Jesus is real we have fellowship with him. We can hear him and see him with the eyes of our hearts and our souls. And through him, we have fellowship with God the Father. In Jesus we hear, see, and experience the Father. We know God. We live in an intimate relationship with him. This is eternal life. This is the deeper life.

This fellowship is the outcome of the person and work of Jesus Christ. When we believe and accept Jesus as Lord and Savior, we become part of the body of Christ. We are placed in fellowship with God and other believers.

Fellowship is the common participation of all believers in the grace of God, the salvation of Christ, and the indwelling of the Holy Spirit.[7] This makes us one. This gives us joy in this life. We can live the deeper life with joy.

Of course, in this life, this fellowship is still partial, and the joy is incomplete. Some pull away from the fellowship (1 John 2:19). Some run ahead (2 John 9). Some cannot love (1 John 4:20). Some will not acknowledge Jesus as real (4:2-3). And so the community is broken. We live in a hurting and broken world.[8]

When there are disagreements within the church, the great temptation is to withdraw, to go somewhere else for fellowship, or to split the church. By doing that we allow worldly and selfish values to influence our decisions. Every fellowship is flawed, imperfect, and in the process of being formed. Instead of running away to find the perfect fellowship, we are called to love, to dialogue, to reason together, to make peace, and to work for unity.

In doing this, we build up one another helping each other toward perfection. Then our joy will be greater and become complete. In this way, we learn to live the deeper life together, in fellowship with one another. Our fellowship with one another reflects the fellowship we have with God.

When we experience this fellowship we know that we are living the deeper life. As we journey with John we will learn more ways in which we can know that we are living the deeper life.

This is the kingdom way—the way of love, in fellowship with God the Father, the Son, and the Holy Spirit, and with one another. We must be God's peculiar people in the world. When we live the kingdom life of love, we build bridges, restore relationships, and work for unity. "Blessed are the peacemakers for they will be called children of God" (Matthew 5:9). This fellowship gives us a new model for human relationships. The deeper life is living out this fellowship in love and peace. We must not allow divisions to destroy this fellowship. We can show the world that there is a better way—the way of love in fellowship with God the Father, the Son, and the Holy Spirit.

Above all, our Lord, who is real, is the Lord of our fellowship, and he is present in our fellowship.

We can live the deeper life because Jesus is real. This is the only way to live, the way of Jesus. We are in Christ, and Christ is in us. Therefore, we can live as Jesus did. Christ living in us is not dependent on our faith or our feelings. He is with us, living in us even when we do not feel his presence. This is a mystery but also the truth. The deeper life is to accept and live this truth. Our God is alive! And He lives in us. Therefore, we can live the Christian life with love, joy, peace, and confidence.

REFLECTION

1. What are your beliefs about Jesus? Who is Jesus for you?

ACTION

1. Stop and become silent for five minutes. Do this now, before you read further. Pause your thoughts. Focus your mind on Jesus. Become aware of him, of his presence with you. To help, envision in your mind a picture of Jesus sitting next to you,

looking at you, talking with you. Do not overthink this. Just be quiet in his presence. He is there! He is with you! Just sit, rest, and be with him. Do this for at least five minutes. Repeat this exercise daily during your devotional time, or any other time where and when you can pause your life and thoughts, and just spend time in his presence.

---

1. See C.S. Keener, "The Gospel of John and the Johannine Letters," in *Faithlife Study Bible*, ed. J.D. Barry (Bellingham, WA: Lexham Press, 2012, 2016).
2. This explanation based on B. Witherington, III, *NT221 The Wisdom of John: A Socio-Rhetorical Commentary on Johannine Literature*, (Bellingham, WA: Lexham Press, 2014). See this resource for a more detailed explanation of this rhetoric and John's style.
3. For the sources used here and a detailed discussion of the context and purpose of First John see:
    J.D. Barry, et al., 2012, 2016. *Faithlife Study Bible*, (Bellingham, WA: Lexham Press, 2012, 2106); B. Witherington, III, *NT221 The Wisdom of John: A Socio-Rhetorical Commentary on Johannine Literature*, (Bellingham, WA: Lexham Press, 2014); the ESV Literary Study Bible; the HSBC Apologetics Study Bible; and the NIV Life Application Study Bible.
4. Paraphrased from the lyrics of the song by Newsboys, "Guilty," on *Love Riot*, released March 4, 2016, Newsboys Inc.
5. See Johannes P. Louw & Eugene A. Nida, eds., *Greek-English lexicon of the New Testament: based on semantic domains*, 2nd ed. (New York: United Bible Societies, 1996), 1, 278; and also Hortz R. Balz & Gerhard Schneider, *Exegetical dictionary of the New Testament*, (Edinburgh: T & T Clark,1990), 2, 136.
6. See John 20:27-29 and Luke 24:39.
7. See J.E. McDermond, *1, 2, 3 John*, (Harrisonburg, VA; Waterloo, ON: Herald Press, 2011), 51.
8. McDermond, *1, 2, 3 John*, 54.

4
FELLOWSHIP WITH GOD

"This is the message we have heard from him and declare to you: God is light; in him, there is no darkness at all. If we claim to have fellowship with him and yet walk in the darkness, we lie and do not live out the truth. But if we walk in the light, as he is in the light, we have fellowship with one another, and the blood of Jesus, his Son, purifies us from all sin.

"If we claim to be without sin, we deceive ourselves and the truth is not in us. If we confess our sins, he is faithful and just and will forgive us our sins and purify us from all unrighteousness. If we claim we have not sinned, we make him out to be a liar and his word is not in us.

"My dear children, I write this to you so that you will not sin. But if anybody does sin, we have an advocate with the Father—Jesus Christ, the Righteous One. He is the atoning sacrifice for our sins and not only for ours but also for the sins of the whole world." (1 John 1:5-2:2)

IN THE PREVIOUS CHAPTER, we learned that the deeper life is having fellowship with God and one another. But to have fellowship with God we must walk in the light. How can we walk in the light and have fellowship with God and one another? This is what this passage in John is about.

In the previous passage, 1 John 1:1-4, John gave evidence that

Jesus Christ is the truth and that the gospel message is true. He continues, "This is the message we have heard from him and declare to you." They heard it straight from Jesus, the Son of God. What is this message?

1. God is Light

"God is light, in him there is no darkness at all."

Here, darkness represents all that is bad, sinful, and evil. Light represents what is good, pure, holy, true, and reliable.[1] God is light. That is, God is completely, perfectly holy, righteous, and true. It is impossible for us as humans to explain the holiness of God. It is beyond words and our imagination.

When Moses encountered God in the burning bush, he wanted to run away, to escape from being involved in God's mission to save his people. When Isaiah saw God in the temple, he feared for his life. Peter met Jesus and told him to go away because he (Peter) was a sinner. When John saw the risen Jesus, he fell at his feet as though dead.[2]

I know this, that when we encounter the holy God, we will be so overwhelmed by his holiness and glory, that like the elders, the angels, and the living creatures around God's throne, we will fall down before God and say, "Holy, holy, holy is the Lord God Almighty."[3]

Light and darkness cannot exist together. The one drives out the other. Where there is darkness, there is no light. And in the dark, you cannot distinguish between things, between good and bad. But where there is light, the darkness is driven away. And the light makes everything visible, exposes whatever exists, shows them for what they are, whether good or bad.[4]

In the same way, sin cannot exist or survive in the holy presence of God. God's holiness and righteousness cannot tolerate sin. It must be destroyed in his holy presence. Sin must be punished. If not, then God is not holy, righteous, and just. That is why only

Jesus, the Son of God, can save us. Only he is completely holy, righteous, perfect, and sinless. His blood purified us from all sin, makes us holy so we can enter into the presence of the holy God.

2. Fellowship with God

In verse 6, John says, "If we claim to have fellowship with him and yet walk in the darkness, we lie and do not live out the truth."

Here he counters the false teachers who said it is possible to have fellowship with God and continue living in sin. They claimed that sin does not break your relationship with God. Sin does not matter. The false teachers believed that what is important is the spirit. The body is evil and worthless. They gave themselves over to worldly desires and greed, gratifying every physical lust. To them, this was acceptable because they believed the body would be destroyed anyway.[5]

Similar teachings appear today in all kinds of spiritualities and practices. They promote the view that it's okay to live for yourself. Enjoy life and fulfill your desires as you wish. These teachings tell us to chase our dreams and achieve them in any way possible, even if that involves questionable practices. Some say, "Don't worry about sin." They say this because Jesus is the atoning sacrifice for all our sins—past, present, and future. So, if God is going to forgive us anyway, we might as well go on sinning.

But we cannot have fellowship with God when we walk in the darkness, because there cannot be fellowship between righteousness and wickedness. Light cannot have fellowship with darkness. We are the temple of the living God. As God has said, "I will live with them and walk among them, and I will be their God, and they will be my people" (2 Cor. 6:14-17). But God cannot live in this temple, in us, when there is darkness. We cannot hide our evil deeds. God's light exposes them. He sees them. He knows. So, if we pretend to have fellowship with God, but walk in the darkness, then we are telling lies.

Think about this. When there is unconfessed sin in your life, or when you persist in sin, how is your relationship and fellowship with God?

It is very hard to have fellowship with God. There seems to be a wall between God and you. It prevents you from experiencing God's presence and love. It prevents you from living and enjoying the deeper life. It takes away the love, joy, peace, confidence, and contentment of living with God every moment.

When you do your devotions, come to church, do ministry, you just go through the motions. Your heart is not in it. The joy is missing. Even if you are trying your best to put your heart into it, something is blocking your fellowship with God.

When we don't deal with sin it erodes our fellowship with God over time. We look for excuses to avoid having fellowship with God. We avoid doing our devotions. We avoid going to church and doing ministry.

Not only is it impossible to have fellowship with God. It is also impossible to have true fellowship with fellow believers. When there is unconfessed sin in our lives, we try to hide it. We fear being rejected. We carry masks. We pretend to be someone we are not. We pretend that everything is good, while it is not. We live a lie. We lie to God, to our fellow believers, and to ourselves.

When we claim that we are children of God, but then live for ourselves, live in darkness, practice evil and immorality, then we do not live and practice the truth. But when we walk in the light, as he is in the light, we have fellowship with God and other believers. Then we are temples of God. He lives with us and in us. He will be our God, he will be our Father, and we will be his children.

Therefore, if we want to have fellowship with God, we must put aside any and all sinful ways of living. How do we do that? We must acknowledge that we are sinners by nature and by deed. We must confess and repent of our sins. And then we must walk in the light.

3. WE ARE SINNERS BY NATURE AND DEED

Humans are sinful by nature. "If we claim to be without sin, we deceive ourselves and the truth is not in us" (verse 8). John counters a second false teaching, which said that humans are not sinful by nature; that people have no natural tendency toward sin.

This false teaching continues today with people who believe that humankind is essentially good. There is no evil in people. These teachings do not take sin seriously. People find all kinds of excuses to explain evil away, or to rationalize sin. When we do this, we deceive ourselves, and the truth is not in us. We deny the truth of God's Word that says no one is without sin.[6] We deny the truth and the evidence of life and historical experience that show how evil and sinful humankind is.

We are also sinners by deed. "If we claim that we have not sinned, we make him out to be a liar, and his word is not in us" (verse 10).

Here, John counters another false teaching. The false teachers denied that they were sinning and that there was any sin in their behavior. This was also a lie. God's Word, which is the truth, tells us that we are sinners and that we do sin. Not only that, the Word—both the Living Word (Jesus) and Scripture—tells us that Jesus came to save us because we are sinners and have sinned. So, if we say that we are without sin and have not sinned, we say God is lying, and we deny the need for Jesus' sacrifice for us. He then died for nothing.

Yes, it is true that God forgives us all our sins—past, present, and future—because of Jesus' atoning sacrifice. His blood purifies us from all sin and unrighteousness. And yet, we still sin after we become Christians. The old sinful nature and the new life, the child of God, are still living together in us. And sometimes, the old self takes over, and we sin. But as a child of God, we know that we have sinned. So what should we do?

4. Confess and Repent

We should confess and repent. "If we confess our sins, he is faithful and just and will forgive us our sins and purify us from all unrighteousness." (verse 9)

Confession and repentance are important for the deeper life. We acknowledge to God and ourselves that we are sinners. We agree with God that our sin is truly sin and that we are willing to turn from it.

Confession brings sin into the light. There is no point in trying to hide those sins. God is light, and he sees our sins. He knows what we have done. Confessing is stating the truth about ourselves, and the truth sets us free. Confession frees us to enjoy full fellowship with God.

When we don't confess our sins, we may become used to the sin. We may even begin to cultivate that sin. And over time, it becomes habit and natural to us. We no longer see it as a sin. And we drift farther and farther away from God.

When we confess our sins, we give up the power of sin over our lives. We repent. We turn away from sin and self. We crucify ourselves. We turn toward the Lord. Jesus re-takes his place as Lord of our lives. We give control back to the Holy Spirit, and we allow the power of the Holy Spirit to work in us to make us holy and change us into children of the light, who have fellowship with God and one another.

It is also important to confess our sins to each other as James 5:16 teaches us: "Therefore, confess your sins to each other and pray for each other so that you may be healed. The prayer of a righteous person is powerful and effective."

When we do not confess to each other, we don't have someone who can pray for us and with us. We don't have someone to encourage us, support us, hold us accountable, and help us overcome sin in our lives. Confessing our sins to each other is an opportunity to love, to forgive, to support, and to encourage each other. Not to judge or reject each other.

I dream of a church, a fellowship of believers, where there is so much love, grace, and trust that we can take off the masks, be vulnerable, submit to one another in love, and confess our sins without fear of being judged, condemned, or rejected. Instead, we come next to the repenting person to pray with them, to encourage them, to help them overcome sin, and grow in Christ. And they do the same for us when we fail, sin and repent. We allow God and others to speak truth into our lives, and help us grow in holiness. We do not fear to confess, to live in the light, because we know there is love, grace, and forgiveness. The truth will set us free, and so enable us to live the deeper life.

5. Jesus Christ is our Advocate

What makes confession and forgiveness possible? What makes it possible for us to walk in the light, to have fellowship with God, with one another, and so to live the deeper life?

Jesus Christ, the Righteous One, is our advocate with the Father. He is the atoning sacrifice for our sins and for the sins of the whole world. His blood purifies us from all sin. Because of his atoning sacrifice, God forgives us our sins and purifies us from all unrighteousness.

We don't have to feel guilty anymore, because we are no longer guilty. We don't have to confess the same sins over and over again unless we repeat them. God is faithful to his promises. God loves us. He wants to forgive us. He does forgive us. God is just. Our debt has been paid by Jesus. Justice has been served. We have been set free. God declared us righteous in Christ.

We don't have to remain stuck in our past lives, no matter how bad or sinful they were. We have been washed clean, completely, from all of our sins. The evilest of deeds, the most vile sins—all are washed away and forgiven. We have a new life in Christ. And Jesus is not just the atoning sacrifice for our sins, but for the sins of the whole world. God's salvation, God's forgiveness, is available for all those who turn from the darkness and enter into the light.

Do you want to live the deeper life with God? All you have to do is believe, repent, confess, receive God's forgiveness, and commit your life to Jesus Christ. And when, as a child of God, you do sin, don't give up, don't go back into the darkness. Confess your sins and experience the joy of forgiveness. And then live with the freedom, joy, peace, confidence, and contentment that comes with walking in the light and living in fellowship with God and with brothers and sisters in Christ.

REFLECTION

1. How is your fellowship with God? With your brothers and sisters in Christ?

ACTION

1. Spend some time in prayer. Allow God's Word and the Holy Spirit to speak to you. Examine your heart. What unconfessed sins are there? Confess them and ask God's forgiveness.

---

1. *NIV Life Application Study Bible*, (Grand Rapids, MI: Zondervan, 2011), 2115.
2. See Ex. 3:1-4:17; Isa. 6:1-5; Luke 5:8; Rev. 1:17.
3. See Rev. 4:8,10-11; 5:9-14.
4. *NIV Life Application Study Bible*, (Grand Rapids, MI: Zondervan, 2011), 2115.
5. *NIV Life Application Study Bible*, 2115.
6. See Prov. 20:9; Jer. 2:35; Rom. 3:9-19; Jas. 3:2

5
LIVING THE JESUS LIFE—BELIEVE AND OBEY (PART 1)

"We know that we have come to know him if we keep his commands. Whoever says, 'I know him,' but does not do what he commands is a liar, and the truth is not in that person. But if anyone obeys his word, love for God is truly made complete in them. This is how we know we are in him: Whoever claims to live in him must live as Jesus did.

"Dear friends, I am not writing you a new command but an old one, which you have had since the beginning. This old command is the message you have heard. Yet I am writing you a new command; its truth is seen in him and in you, because the darkness is passing and the true light is already shining.

"Anyone who claims to be in the light but hates a brother or sister is still in the darkness. Anyone who loves their brother and sister lives in the light, and there is nothing in them to make them stumble. But anyone who hates a brother or sister is in the darkness and walks around in the darkness. They do not know where they are going, because the darkness has blinded them." (1 John 2:3-11)

LET'S begin this chapter by asking some questions. These are questions John's churches asked as they faced false teachings and divisions. We are dealing with the same questions today as we try to follow Jesus faithfully in this world:

- How do we know that we know God?
- How do we know that our Christian faith is authentic?
- How can we be sure that we belong to Christ?
- How do we know that we are living the new, deeper life?
- How do we know that we are truly following Jesus and that this is not just a game, the Jesus-game or church-game, we are playing?

Reflect for a while on these questions before you read on. Write down your thoughts if you wish.

AS JOHN ANSWERS THESE QUESTIONS IN THIS PASSAGE, HE introduces four themes, which he come back to repeatedly, each time going deeper and expanding on them:

(1) knowing God (verses 3-4);

(2) obedience (verses 3-8);

(3) eschatology, that is the teachings on the end times and Jesus' return,[1] (verse 8); and

(4) loving one another. (verses 9-11)[2]

In these verses, he gives us tests and evidence, by which we can know whether we know God. In verses 3-6, he gives us a general test—we know God if we obey his commands. He interrupts himself briefly in verses 7-8 to talk about the old and new commandments. And then in verses 9-11, he gives us a specific test—we know God if we love others.[3]

Thus, the short answer to these questions is:

We know that we know God when we obey his commands by loving others.

We know that we are in Christ, when we live as Jesus did. Those who believe, obey and love; and those who obey and love, believe.[4] Let's look at this in more depth.

1. Do you know God? Do you know Jesus?

When we ask the question, "Do you know God?" we are also asking, "Do you know Jesus?" We can only know God if we know Jesus, because Jesus is God. And we can only know God the Father through Jesus because Jesus is the Son of God. Jesus said, "I am the way and the truth and the life. No one comes to the Father except through me. If you really know me, you will know my Father as well. From now on, you do know him and have seen him." (John 14:6-7)

How do we know that we know Jesus?

"We know that we have come to know him if we keep his commands." (1 John 2: 3)

We come to know Jesus in uniquely different ways producing in us a special kind of knowledge. This is certain, intimate, relational knowledge that we live out by doing Jesus' commands.

First, we know that something is accurate or certain. Jesus is real and alive as we have seen in chapter three. We know this as truth. Therefore, we can be sure that we know God because of Jesus Christ who came, who lived and died, was resurrected, and now rules as the Risen King and lives in us.

Second, we know because we live in an intimate, close relationship with God through Jesus. This is not just head knowledge. This is not just a statement of faith or abstract theological teaching that we affirm with our minds and reason. This is a relationship of love. This is certain, complete knowledge, knowing Jesus with our whole being—with our hearts, with our heads, and with our hands.

We know with our hands because we live out this knowledge through our actions. We know that we know Jesus, that we are living the deeper life and loving God when we obey his commands and live as Jesus lived.

What are his commands? They are summarized in 1 John

3:23-24, where the heart of these commands is stated like this: "And this is his command: to believe in the name of his Son, Jesus Christ, and to love one another as he commanded us. The one who keeps God's commands lives in him, and he in them."

Believe and love. Believe and obey. Believe and do. Believe and live the Jesus-life. To know Jesus is to abide in Him, to have union with Christ—Christ in us, and we in Christ.[5]

If our faith is authentic, if we truly believe that Jesus is the Son of God and the Lord of our lives, then we will obey him. We will live like him. And, when we live as Jesus did, then we come to know him better. Our relationship with him grows deeper, and our love for him increases. We fall in love with him more and more.

That is why John says in 1 John 2:5, that the one who obeys his word, in that person the love of God is perfected, made complete, matures, and reaches its goal. This means that as God's love fills us, our love for God increases. Our love for others increases as we love them with God's love. We love and serve them and so become channels of God's love to the world. Obedience flows out of and is the result of our love for God, and his love for us.

There are no compromises, no "but's," with John or Jesus. 1 John 2:4—"Whoever says, 'I know him' but does not do what he commands is a liar, and the truth is not in that person." Just read what Jesus says in the gospel of John in chapters, 8, 14, 15:

> *Jesus said to them, "If God were your Father, you would love me, for I have come here from God. I have not come on my own; God sent me. Why is my language not clear to you? Because you are unable to hear what I say. You belong to your father, the devil, and you want to carry out your father's desires. He was a murderer from the beginning, not holding to the truth, for there is no truth in him. When he lies, he speaks his native language, for he is a liar and the father of lies. Yet because I tell the truth, you do not believe me! Can any of you prove me guilty of sin? If I am telling the truth, why don't you believe me? Whoever*

belongs to God hears what God says. The reason you do not hear is that you do not belong to God." ... "Very truly I tell you, whoever obeys my word will never see death." (John 8:42-47,51)

"Very truly I tell you, whoever believes in me will do the works I have been doing, and they will do even greater things than these, because I am going to the Father. ... If you love me, keep my commands. ... Whoever has my commands and keeps them is the one who loves me. The one who loves me will be loved by my Father, and I too will love them and show myself to them." ... Jesus replied, "Anyone who loves me will obey my teaching. My Father will love them, and we will come to them and make our home with them. Anyone who does not love me will not obey my teaching. These words you hear are not my own; they belong to the Father who sent me." (John 14:12,15,21,23-24)

"I am the vine; you are the branches. If you remain in me and I in you, you will bear much fruit; apart from me, you can do nothing. If you do not remain in me, you are like a branch that is thrown away and withers; such branches are picked up, thrown into the fire and burned. If you remain in me and my words remain in you, ask whatever you wish, and it will be done for you. This is to my Father's glory, that you bear much fruit, showing yourselves to be my disciples. As the Father has loved me, so have I loved you. Now remain in my love. If you keep my commands, you will remain in my love, just as I have kept my Father's commands and remain in his love. I have told you this so that my joy may be in you and that your joy may be complete. My command is this: Love each other as I have loved you. Greater love has no one than this: to lay down one's life for one's friends. You are my friends if you do what I command." (John 15:5-14)

Take note of Jesus' words in Matthew 7:15-23, "Not everyone

who says to me, 'Lord, Lord,' will enter the kingdom of heaven, but only the one who does the will of my Father in heaven." Look also at these verses from Matthew:

1. "Therefore anyone who sets aside one of the least of these commands and teaches others accordingly will be called least in the kingdom of heaven, but whoever practices and teaches these commands will be called great in the kingdom of heaven." (5:19)
2. "Why do you ask me about what is good?" Jesus replied. "There is only One who is good. If you want to enter life, keep the commandments." (19:17)
3. "Woe to you, teachers of the law and Pharisees, you hypocrites! You give a tenth of your spices—mint, dill and cumin. But you have neglected the more important matters of the law—justice, mercy and faithfulness. You should have practiced the latter, without neglecting the former." (23:23)

It is possible for someone's faith not to be authentic. Today, as in John's time, there are many who claim to know God but live sinful lives. Titus 1:16 says, "They claim to know God, but by their actions they deny him. They are detestable, disobedient and unfit for doing anything good."

It is easy to say, "I believe in Jesus; I know Jesus," but it doesn't come from the heart. People say this for various reasons. To escape persecution or death. To get family or friends out of their hair. To get the Bible bashers off their backs. Some want to have what the Christians have, but they want it for selfish reasons. They do not understand or are not willing to pay the costs of discipleship.

Because this is not a true, authentic faith, they do not bear fruit. They do not obey because they have not experienced the amazing grace of Jesus being their Savior or made him the Lord of their life. They are their own lords. They do not care about the Lord's commands, and therefore, they do not live as Jesus did. Some may even go through the motions of being a follower of Jesus. They may even go to church and participate in church ministries. But as soon as they leave the church, they push Jesus off the throne and climb back onto the throne of their lives. They are liars, and the truth is not in them.

I am not talking here about the occasional mistakes, relapses, or moments of disobedience when one's ego takes over. No, this is about persistently living in the darkness and thereby persisting in our old ways, the old life and in sin. We cannot say that we know him, and then live as we like, pursuing our own desires or will. If we continue to sin, we do not know him. (1 John 3:6)

If we do not love, we do not know God. (1 John 4:8) 1 John 2:9-11 states clearly that anyone who hates a brother or sister and therefore disobeys the Lord's commands is still in darkness, walks around in the darkness, and the darkness has blinded them. When Jesus, who is the Light, shines in us, how can we still live in darkness? No, we are called to believe and to obey. We are called to obey his commands, which are ...

2. Old but also New

The Great Commandment to love is old because it is part of God's law for his people and comes from the Old Testament:

1. "Love the LORD your God with all your heart and with all your soul and with all your strength." (Deut. 6:5)
2. "Do not seek revenge or bear a grudge against anyone among your people, but love your neighbor as yourself. I am the LORD." (Lev. 19:18)

The Great Commandment is the summary of all the commandments. It is also old because the believers heard it from the beginning. It was part of the gospel they heard, and Jesus taught this great commandment, see Matthew 22:36-40: "Love the Lord your God with all your heart and with all your soul and with all your mind. This is the first and greatest commandment. And the second is like it: Love your neighbor as yourself. All the Law and the Prophets hang on these two commandments."

But this commandment is also new because Jesus interpreted and lived it in a radically new way:

1. John 13: 34, 35—"A new command I give you: Love one another. As I have loved you, so you must love one another. By this everyone will know that you are my disciples, if you love one another."
2. John 15:13—"Greater love has no one than this: to lay down one's life for one's friends. You are my friends if you do what I command."

Jesus showed us how the old command had been made new and was fulfilled in his life. He obeyed and lived out the command. This love is a self-sacrificing love that entails selfless giving, caring about, and looking out for the good and the well-being of others. This love is willing to give up one's own rights and privileges for the sake of others. Love is servanthood—serving like Jesus did and being willing to die for the other. And if that is not radical enough, Jesus made it even more radical. Selfless, self-giving love is not just for family, friends, and fellow believers. Jesus applies and extends this love to our enemies and persecutors.

> *"You have heard that it was said, 'Love your neighbor and hate your enemy.' But I tell you, love your enemies and pray for those who persecute you, that you may be children of your Father in heaven. He causes his sun to rise on the evil and the good and sends rain on the righteous and the unrighteous. If you love those who love you, what reward will you get? Are not even the tax collectors doing that? And if*

you greet only your own people, what are you doing more than others? Do not even pagans do that? Be perfect, therefore, as your heavenly Father is perfect." (Matt. 5:43-48)

Love must "be the unifying force and the identifying mark of the Christian community. Love is the key to walking in the light because we cannot grow spiritually while we hate others."[6] Our growing relationship with God, our growing knowledge of God, our increasing love for God, our abiding in Christ, will result in us living the Jesus-life. We will follow Jesus' example of complete obedience to God the Father, and therefore, we will obey Jesus' teachings and commands. We will follow Jesus' example of self-giving love and loving service to others. We will believe and obey.

The truth of this new command, of love, is seen in Jesus. Jesus is the true light of the world that gives light to everyone. He came into the world (John 1:9), and because of him, the darkness is passing. Love has been fully realized in Christ. Its truth is also seen in us. In Jesus, we became children of the light. We are now light in the Lord, and therefore, must live as children of the light, and the fruit of the light is goodness, righteousness, and truth. (Eph. 5:8)

1 Thessalonians 5:5 says, "You are all children of the light and children of the day. We do not belong to the night or to the darkness." Jesus, the Light, lives in us, and we are in him. And as we become like him, his light is shining in the world through us more and more. We are the light of the world.

But is all this possible? Is the deeper life possible? Is change possible? Earlier, I mentioned the gap between what Christians claim is true about themselves, and what we often see when we look at ourselves and others. Many who claim to have Christ, are not living in the light as children of God. Christians who are supposed to be set apart by their love, are not known for love.[7] The life the Bible describes looks so different from the lives many Christians are living. What's wrong? What should we do?

Believe and obey. And here the problem lies. Faith and works; grace and deeds. There is a tension here. Many see these two elements as opposing and excluding each other. Today, as in John's time, we have two voices, two views, two ways. The first, the way of extravagant grace, says, "Just believe." The other, the way of radical discipleship, says, "Just obey."[8]

For Jesus, and John, it is not "either-or" but "both-and." You cannot separate these two. Believe and obey. We live out our faith through obedience, and obedience is the fruit of our faith. But what does that really mean? What is the relationship between these two? We will look at that in depth in the next chapter.

For now, remember this—Living the abundant, deeper, new life is to live the Jesus-life through faith and obedience. And we can live this life with confidence because we are in Christ and Christ is in us. By the power of the Spirit we believe, we obey, we know God, we love God, and we love others. When we love others, we live in the light as God is in the light, and we have fellowship with God. Then we know and love God.

Reflection

1. How well do you know Jesus? To help you answer this question think about the following questions—Who is Jesus? What does Jesus mean for you? How would you describe, explain, or introduce Jesus as your best friend to someone else?

Action

1. What can you do to know Jesus better? Do that for one week.
2. Identify one thing, one area of life, or one teaching of Jesus that you are not obeying. Pray about that. Confess your disobedience about that one thing. Repent, and decide to obey Jesus in

that one thing. Pray for the power of the Holy Spirit to help you. Then go and do it.[9]

---

1. Eschatology is the study of the end times and the second coming of Jesus Christ. It refers to the biblical teachings about the new age that has begun with Christ's first coming, the old age that is passing, and the new age that will be completed or fulfilled with his second coming.
2. See J. E. McDermond, *1, 2, 3 John*, Believers Church Bible Commentary (Harrisonburg, VA; Waterloo, ON: Herald Press, 2011), 83.
3. J.E. McDermond, *1, 2, 3 John*, 84.
4. Adapted from Bonhoeffer's statements "'Only those who believe obey' ... and 'only those who obey believe' ... Only those who obey can believe, and only those who believe can obey" in Dietrich Bonhoeffer, *The Cost of Discipleship* (New York: Collier-Macmillan, 1963), 74, 76, quoted by Wilbourne, *Union*, Kindle loc 810.
5. Wilbourne, Kindle loc 439.
6. *NIV Life Application Study Bible*, (Grand Rapids, MI: Zondervan, 2011), 2116.
7. Wilbourne, Kindle Loc 669.
8. These phrases come from and these two ways are described by Wilbourne, Kindle Loc 675.
9. For this chapter I am indebted to the following two sources: (1) J.E. McDermond, *1, 2, 3 John*, (Harrisonburg, VA; Waterloo, ON: Herald Press, 2011); and (2) Rankin Wilbourne, *Union with Christ: The Way to Know and Enjoy God* (Colorado Springs, CO: David C Cook, 2016), Kindle loc 654-657. I give full credit to them for the ideas, the reasoning and outline I used in this chapter, especially Wilbourne. His book, ideas, and thinking were a major help and resource, not just for this chapter, but as already stated in my Acknowledgement, for this whole book.

6

LIVING THE JESUS LIFE—BELIEVE AND OBEY! (PART 2)

"We know that we have come to know him if we keep his commands. Whoever says, 'I know him,' but does not do what he commands is a liar, and the truth is not in that person. But if anyone obeys his word, love for God is truly made complete in them. This is how we know we are in him: Whoever claims to live in him must live as Jesus did.

"Dear friends, I am not writing you a new command but an old one, which you have had since the beginning. This old command is the message you have heard. Yet I am writing you a new command; its truth is seen in him and in you, because the darkness is passing and the true light is already shining.

"Anyone who claims to be in the light but hates a brother or sister is still in the darkness. Anyone who loves their brother and sister lives in the light, and there is nothing in them to make them stumble. But anyone who hates a brother or sister is in the darkness and walks around in the darkness. They do not know where they are going, because the darkness has blinded them." (1 John 2:3-11)

WE ARE STILL CAMPING out in 1 John 2:3-11. We are trying to answer these questions—How do we know that we know God? How do we know that our Christian faith is authentic? How do we know that we are truly following Jesus? How do we know that we are living the new, deeper life?

Let's look at the relationship between faith and obedience in more depth. To follow Jesus, we must believe in Jesus Christ as our Lord and Savior, *and* we must obey Jesus Christ as our Lord and Savior.

1. Believe ... more?

We are saved by grace "through faith—and this is not from ourselves, it is the gift of God—not by works, so that no one can boast." (Eph 2:8-10) God loves us unconditionally, so much so that he gave his Son Jesus to save us. Jesus is our Savior. It is all amazing grace, and we have done nothing to earn or deserve it. All we need to do to make this salvation, this new life, real in our lives is to believe—to believe that Jesus the Christ is the Lord and Savior. We accept this gift of salvation through faith. We believe that in Christ Jesus we have new, eternal life. And the Holy Spirit makes this new life real in us, changing us to become like Christ.

But then, we still see people who say they believe, but their lives are not changing. We cannot ignore Jesus' important and strong statement that not everyone who calls him Lord will enter the kingdom but the one who obeys. (Matt. 7:21) And what do we do with these words from Hebrews 12:14, "Make every effort to live in peace with everyone and to be holy. Without holiness, no one will see the Lord."

Yes, it is all grace and faith only. We must believe. We do believe. But there is a real danger of cheap grace.

Dietrich Bonhoeffer in his book *The Cost of Discipleship* explains this well:

Cheap grace is the deadly enemy of our Church. Cheap grace means ... the preaching of forgiveness without requiring repentance ... grace without discipleship, grace without the cross ... Those who try to use grace as a dispensation from following Christ are simply deceiving them-

selves ... We confess that, although our Church is orthodox as far as her doctrine of grace is concerned, we are no longer sure that we are members of a church which follows its Lord.[1]

"Cheap grace can become an excuse not to follow Jesus. It can cause people to rest secure in their ungodly living. Cheap grace works without asking anything from us."[2]

Dallas Willard talks about the same problem in two excellent books, *The Divine Conspiracy* and *The Great Omission*. He calls discipleship "The Great Omission" in the church today. People use grace to excuse and avoid discipleship. And thereby they reduce the gospel. They take out the important call to follow Jesus, and to learn from Jesus how to live the Jesus-life in the Kingdom of God in this life.[3] The gospel is reduced to what Willard calls "a gospel of sin management."[4] We have reduced life with God to a barcode faith "wherein simply by our verbal confession, we exchange our sins for Christ's righteousness, and thereby acquire our ticket for heaven when this life is over."[5]

This teaching of cheap grace says, "Jesus is our Savior, but not the Lord of our life." Cheap grace silences Jesus' call for us to follow him. But there are no ifs, ands, or buts with Jesus. "If you love me, you will keep my commandments" (John 14:15) and, "You are my friends if you do what I command you." (John 15:14)

Bonhoeffer also said, "The only man who has a right to say that he is justified by grace alone is the man who has left all to follow Christ."[6] The only way to know God is to follow Jesus. We are called to come and die, to take up our crosses. To obey Jesus.[7]

2. Obey ... More?

But here we have another real danger, the danger of salvation through works. It is the idea that we can somehow earn our salvation through obedience. So, some people obey out of fear of punishment (hell) or to earn some kind of reward (heaven). They think you must follow the rules to be called Christian and to be saved.

Have you tried to follow and obey Jesus and then failed? You want to live the Jesus-life, a holy life, but it seems as if your life is not changing? So, you try harder: "I will obey Jesus more." And nothing changes. Try harder; obey more. We are disappointed because we fail. We cannot do it. And soon we become discouraged and exhausted from trying. Some become cynical and skeptical. Some even give up.

When talking about the deeper life, I have this fear that some may become discouraged, cynical, or skeptical. They may say, "Well, it all sounds good, but it's not possible to live and experience the new, deeper life in Christ. It's only for some, for the super spiritual."

Please do not become discouraged. I hope that this book will show you that the deeper life is for everyone. It is real, and possible, not because of our will power or our own strength, but because of the power of the Holy Spirit.

What is obedience? In the Bible, obedience is not just knowing the commands. To obey (according to John) means doing. A literal translation of 1 John 5:2 could be, "We do his commandments." We make them part of our life and do them.

Why do we obey? Out of fear? For a reward? Or do we obey because we love God? Because we are in awe of God's grace and love for us?

3. Follow Jesus—Believe and Obey!

How do we hold these two together—the gospel of extravagant grace that requires nothing from us, and the gospel of radical discipleship that asks everything of us?[8] Is it a question of balance? No, because balance means a 50/50 split, a compromise, and we need 100 percent of both.[9] "Only those who obey can believe, and only those who believe can obey."[10] We must hold both together. But how?

We are in Christ, Christ is in us, and he has truly made himself one with us. It is because of this union with Christ, that grace and discipleship, faith and obedience come together in our lives.[11] Wilbourne states in his book, *Union with Christ*:

> *The problem with either 'just believe the gospel ... more' or 'just obey your Lord ... more' is that alone, they leave us focusing on ourselves as the agent of change. There's something we need to do. Either ... by itself, places us at the center. But union with Christ displaces us from the center of our own lives.*[12]

When we believe, Jesus comes and lives in us. Joyful obedience grows out of this union, this intimate and dynamic relationship. The power of the Holy Spirit empowers us to obey. But for this to happen, we must make sure that we are in Christ. That we remain in Him. Abide in Him. We will discuss later how we do this.

But now you may say, "I believe, but I continue to struggle with disobedience. Does that mean my faith is not real?"

If we truly believe but persist in sin, then we must examine our hearts. The problem is that we are not abiding in Christ. He is in us, but we are not in him. In such a case, something prevents us from abiding in Christ; from allowing Him to fully be Lord of our lives. It could be pride, lust, envy, not practicing the spiritual disciplines, not yielding to the Holy Spirit, or some unconfessed sin.

Pray. Talk with a fellow believer. Find what prevents you from truly or fully abiding in Christ. Repent, confess, believe, abide in Christ, and obey.

What happens when a fellow brother or sister persists in disobedience. Is their faith false?

We cannot judge. Only God knows a person's heart. But we are called to help that person—to call them to repentance. Not to judge or condemn them. We must come right up next to them and help them to discover what is wrong. We must love them, and when they repent, extend grace and forgive them.

Only when they ignore or reject our admonition and persist

in sin do we go the way of church discipline as explained in Matthew 18:15-20. But even then, remember that the purpose of church discipline is not to judge and punish people, but to bring them to repentance and to restore them. Church discipline must be rooted in, driven by, and guided by love. And only after repeated efforts by the whole church body to bring that member to repentance, and with no change, will we take the extreme step of cutting him or her off from the body of Christ.

Our old self is still living in us and fighting for control of our souls. I think that sometimes our focus is too much on the old self and not on the new self: Christ in us. We are so focused on our sins, that we don't see how the Holy Spirit is changing us. We need to live more in the awareness of the reality that we are children of God and are filled with the Holy Spirit. We are living and growing into the new life we have in Christ.

Look at your life, past and present. Have you changed? Does your life look different?

Of course, it does.

Look at your life now. Is it changing? Are you growing?

Of course, you are.

If you say "No," then you are denying the presence, the work, and the power of the Holy Spirit in your life.

And when you disobey your Lord, what happens? How do you feel? Happy, joyful, content?

No, you are contrite, you are grieved, you feel sad, you are sorry, and your soul is in pain. But do you give up? Do you wallow in sorrow?

No, we repent and go back to our Lord. We confess our sins and receive his forgiveness. And we go on with confidence because Christ is in us, and we are in him.

We must learn to trust that God is at work in our lives through his Holy Spirit. We need to pay attention and take notice of where and how God is working in our lives. We should take courage from that. We should encourage one another when we see how God is working in their lives. We should encourage and help one another to abide in Christ.

The Christian music band, Newsboys, sings these words, "My God's not dead. He is surely alive. He is living inside me."[13]

And because of God living inside us, we can live the Jesus-life with confidence and joy through faith and obedience. When we *believe in* and *obey* Jesus Christ as Lord and Savior, we accept Jesus and his Holy Spirit into our lives. Jesus, through the power of his Spirit, changes us to become like him and live the Jesus-life.

REFLECTION

1. Has cheap grace or salvation by works played a role in your Christian life? In what ways?

2. What questions do you still have about faith and obedience?

ACTION

1. What do you need to change in your views, attitude, and life to experience extravagant grace and practice radical discipleship? Identify one thing and try to make that change.

2. Talk with a fellow believer, a spiritual friend, or mentor about this, and ask them to help you.[14]

---

1. Dietrich Bonhoeffer, *The Cost of Discipleship* (New York: Collier-Macmillan, 1963), 45, 47, 55, 60. quoted by Wilbourne, *Union*, Kindle loc 761-764.
2. Brennan Manning, *All Is Grace: A Ragamuffin Memoir* (Colorado Springs: David C Cook, 2011), 194, quoted by Wilbourne, Kindle loc 765.
3. Dallas Willard, *The Great Omission: Rediscovering Jesus' Essential Teachings on Discipleship* (San Francisco: HarperOne, 2006), 226, quoted and discussed by Wilbourne, Kindle loc 782-785.
4. Dallas Willard, *The Divine Conspiracy: Rediscovering Our Hidden Life in God* (San Francisco: HarperSanFrancisco, 1998), 41, 37, quoted and discussed by Wilbourne, Kindle loc 782-785.

5. Wibourne, Kindle loc 784 quoting and referring to Willard, *The Divine Conspiracy*, 37.
6. Bonhoeffer, *The Cost of Discipleship*, 55, quoted by Wilbourne, Kindle loc 767-768.
7. See Wilbourne, Kindle loc 793.
8. Wilbourne, Kindle loc 675.
9. Wilbourne, Kindle loc 806.
10. Bonhoeffer, 74, 76, quoted by Wilbourne, Kindle loc 810.
11. Wilbourne, Kindle loc 825
12. Wilbourne, Kindle loc 832-836.
13. Newsboys, "God's Not Dead," on *God's Not Dead*, released November 11, 2011, Inpop Records.
14. For this chapter I again give full credit to the following authors and sources.. (1) J.E. McDermond, 1, 2, 3 John, (Harrisonburg, VA; Waterloo, ON: Herald Press, 2011); and (2) Rankin Wilbourne, *Union with Christ: The Way to Know and Enjoy God* (Colorado Springs, CO: David C Cook, 2016), Ch.3, Kindle loc 654-919. This chapter is especially based on and follow the ideas, thinking, and outline of Wilbourne's chapter 3

7
WE HAVE OVERCOME

"I am writing to you, dear children, because your sins have been forgiven on account of his name. I am writing to you, fathers, because you know him who is from the beginning.

"I am writing to you, young men, because you have overcome the evil one.

"I write to you, dear children, because you know the Father. I write to you, fathers, because you know him who is from the beginning. I write to you, young men, because you are strong, and the word of God lives in you, and you have overcome the evil one." (1 John 2:12-14)

THE DEEPER LIFE is living the new life in Christ with love, joy, peace, confidence, and contentment as we live every moment with God. What does it mean to live the new life with confidence? How can we do that?

In this passage, John writes to give his readers assurance and encouragement.[1] First, he assures them that they are in Christ. They are not like the false teachers. They are not like the people who left the church or like those who try to divide the church. Their sins are forgiven. They know Jesus and the Father. They are strong, and the Word of God lives in them. They have overcome evil. They have victory in Christ, and they have no need for these false teachings, lies, or the desires of the world.

With these words of assurance, however, John also reminds them that the fact that they have victory and new life in Jesus Christ does not mean that they can now sit back and do nothing. In the next passages, John tells them that they must continue to resist the world and the evil one. They must work out their salvation and live out their faith through obedience. They can live this new life with confidence because they have overcome.

These words of assurance and encouragement are also meant for us today as we live the new life. We also have overcome! But not because of our own efforts or by our own strength. It is all God's work for us and in us. It is because of Christ's victory, and because of our union with Christ, that we have overcome. Therefore, we can live the new life with confidence.

Before I go on, allow me to explain a few things.[2] John wrote this passage in a special way. Although not poetry, he structured these statements in a poetic way. He did this because he wanted to emphasize the importance of these foundational truths. This passage forms a bridge between the previous passages and what follows.

First, let's look at his audience. He addresses them as children, fathers, and young men. This is a special literary style or technique that we find also in other places in the Bible.[3] He first addresses and identifies the whole group—the whole church. "Children" is the special term of endearment that John uses to address the believers (the church). Then he goes on to identify and address specific groups within the church. Fathers and young men could refer to different age groups or to different stages in spiritual growth and maturity, or both.

Notice the change of tenses here. Verses 12-13 are in the present tense, and verse 14 is in the past tense. This is a literary technique for emphasis. However, John uses the perfect tense for "your sins have been forgiven," "you have known," and "you have overcome." This means that the actions and their effects are ongoing. It's not past tense, finished, and it's not only for some. We can also experience these effects today in our daily lives.

Through John's careful use of language, he emphasizes his main message: We have overcome, therefore, we can live the new life with confidence.

In the next passages, we'll discuss the *how* and the *why*.

1. OUR SINS ARE FORGIVEN

We have overcome because our sins have been forgiven on account of his name—the Son of God, Jesus Christ. Our sins are forgiven, not because of something we did or because of who we are, but because of Jesus. "The blood of Jesus, his Son, purifies us from all sin." (1 John 1:7) "We have an advocate with the Father—Jesus Christ, the Righteous One. He is the atoning sacrifice for our sins." (1 John 2:1-2) We don't need to look for salvation anywhere else. We don't need to take refuge in anything else. We don't need to do something to pay for our sins. Jesus already paid the full price. It is finished! Jesus Christ is our Savior!

This blessed assurance enables us to focus on living the new life we have in Christ. It frees us from self-doubt. It frees us from trying to find fulfillment, satisfaction, meaning, or purpose somewhere else. It frees us from living in the past, from continuing to blame and reprimand ourselves. And yes, we are called to obey and to avoid sin, but this assurance of forgiveness and grace enables us to focus not on our sins but to focus on living in the power of the Holy Spirit. We believe in the name of the Son of God, Jesus Christ. We should fix our eyes on Jesus.

2. WE KNOW JESUS

We have overcome because we know him who is from the beginning. We know Jesus, who is God, the Son of God. He is the Lord and the Creator of the universe. He is eternal. He is the

Alpha and the Omega. All authority in heaven and on earth has been given to him. He holds everything together. He is alive. He is Life. He is Truth. He is real. He is Immanuel, God with us.

We know Jesus because we live in this close, intimate relationship with him. We know him from the beginning. Since we believed, he came and made his home in us. This union with Christ, with the King, makes possible the kingdom life as described by Jesus in the Sermon on the Mount. When we abide in Him, we become like Him, and we live the Jesus-life with confidence.

3. We know the Father

We have overcome because we know the Father. We know the Father because of Jesus. Our sins separate us from the Father. But they are forgiven and are removed because of Jesus. Now we can again be in a close relationship with the Father.

We know the Father because Jesus is the Way to the Father (John 14). Jesus is in the Father, and the Father is in Jesus. Anyone who has seen Jesus has seen the Father. We have experienced Jesus, and in him, we have experienced and come to know the Father.

Because of Jesus, we became children of God. "Yet to all who did receive him, to those who believed in his name, he gave the right to become children of God—children born not of natural descent, nor of human decision or a husband's will, but born of God." (John 1:12-13)

We are children because we are born of the Spirit. The Spirit of God lives in us, and we have a new life because of the Spirit. (Rom. 8:8,11) Those who are "led by the Spirit of God are children of God," and we can call out to God as Father. (Rom. 8:14,15) We can live this new life with confidence because we are children of God, and the Spirit lives in us.

Our Father is the faithful and loving God. His steadfast love endures forever and never fails. This gives us confidence and assurance even in the most difficult situations. We have no need for other gods or idols. We have no need to try all kinds of new age spiritualities to find or experience intimacy with God. We cannot get closer to God than we already are.

The world and the evil one are constantly tempting us to seek joy, pleasure, contentment, confidence, and security in the things of the world. But as we will see in the next passage of First John, these pass away. Any joy they give is fleeting. They never satisfy. Their security is an illusion and disappears overnight. They just cause us to crave more and more. And so, they become our idols.

Young people are tempted today by many temptations to leave the church. They are told that you can follow Jesus on your own terms and in your own way. You don't need the church or even the Bible. Just do good. They are told as long as you fight for social justice, for yourself and others, then you are okay. They are told that all religions and spiritualities are the same—they are different rivers flowing into the same sea.

The young in faith—new believers who are still growing and learning to live the new life—easily doubt the truth and certainty of their salvation. They are vulnerable to the influences of false teachings. John reassures and encourages them, and us, to persevere in living the new Jesus-life.

We can persevere because we find our fulfillment and greatest joy in our fellowship with and worship of God. Not in other gods, idols, religions, spiritualities, or the things of this world.

We can persevere because we have confidence in our salvation and hope. We have this confidence because we know the Father, our God. And our Father is faithful and merciful. His love never fails. He never leaves us alone. He is always with us.

Matt Redman sings these words in his song, *Never Once* —"Knowing that for every step You were with us, Knowing every victory was Your power in us ... with joy our hearts can say, yes, our hearts can say, Never once did we ever walk alone, never once did You leave us on our own. Carried by Your constant grace Held within Your perfect peace. You are faithful, God, You are faithful."[4]

Because of this, we can say with Paul in Philippians 4 that we rejoice in the Lord always, and we are content whatever the circumstances. (verses 4, 11) His power in us gives us the strength to live the new life with confidence.

4. WE ARE STRONG

We have overcome because we are strong. But we are not strong by ourselves. This is not physical strength but spiritual strength. We are strong in the Lord. (Eph. 6:10) We are strong in the Lord because we put on the armor of God every day. The full armor of God enables us to stand and remain standing. (Eph. 6:11-13)

We are strong because the Holy Spirit empowers us. When we live by the power of the Spirit, when we keep in step with the Spirit, we can live the new life with confidence.

We are strong because we pray. Prayer is our first task. We must pray continuously, all the time. We must pray persistently. (Luke 18:1-7) We must pray under all circumstances. (Acts 1:14; 1 Thess. 5:17; Php. 4:4-5) "We must make prayer our life, and our life a prayer."[5] Ephesians 6:18 says, "And pray in the Spirit on all occasions with all kinds of prayers and requests. With this in mind, be alert and always keep on praying for all the Lord's people."

We are strong when we abide in Christ because He lives in us. This is truth, a reality, a fact. This is not a feeling. Christ living in us is not dependent on our feelings. He is there even if we forget about him and don't feel or experience his presence. Many times we pray, "Be with us Lord." But he is already with us. The Word of God lives in us and is with us always. You cannot get closer to God than that.

5. THE WORD OF GOD LIVES IN US

We have overcome because the Word of God lives in us. Jesus Christ, the living Word of God, lives in us through the Holy Spirit. This word is also the message taught and lived by Jesus, the Word of life. And this word is also the written Word of God, the Bible, inspired by the Holy Spirit.

When we are rooted in this Word, living in the Word every day, then we become strong. We overcome, bear fruit, and live the new life.

How do we know Jesus? How do we experience his presence and his power? How do we abide in Christ? Through prayer and through the Bible.

If someone tells me, "I don't hear the voice of God," or, "I don't experience Christ," my response is, "Are you reading the Bible? Are you praying?" I cannot emphasize enough the importance of being in the Word—to study, to read, to meditate, to reflect on, to listen to, and to memorize the Bible. The Word is powerful. The Word is alive and changes us, enabling us to live the new life with confidence.

Don't take my word for it. Believe God's own Word, which says that the word that goes out from God's mouth will not return empty but will accomplish what God desires and achieve the purpose for which he sent it (Is. 55:11). The Lord also declares, "Is not my word like fire...and like a hammer that breaks a rock in pieces." (Jer. 23:29) The Word of God is the sword of the Spirit. "For the word of God is alive and active. Sharper than any double-edged sword, it penetrates even to dividing soul and spirit, joints and marrow; it judges the thoughts and attitudes of the heart." (Heb. 4:12) Deuteronomy 32:47 says, "These words are your life."

The question is: does the Word of God live in us? If we want to live the new life, if we want to know Jesus, if we want to be strong, then we must make sure that we live in and know the Word, and that we abide in Christ. And when the Word lives in us, we will overcome.

6. WE HAVE OVERCOME

The evil one is also real. Don't let the world fool you by telling you that the devil does not exist. He works through, and appears in, those who deny Jesus as the Christ and as the Son of God. "The whole world is under the control of the evil one." (1 John 5:19) He walks around like a lion looking for someone to devour. (1 Pet. 5:8) If he can bring down a child of God, what a victory that will be for him!

So be aware. The new, deeper life gets harder the more we grow in Christ. But, paradoxically, it also becomes easier as we abide in Christ. We have overcome, we are overcoming, and we will overcome because Jesus Christ has already defeated the evil one. "You, dear children, are from God and have overcome them, because the one who is in you is greater than the one who is in the world." (1 John 4:4)

Sometimes we will fail and fall. We are not perfect, but we are being perfected by the Holy Spirit. God's love and faithfulness and grace were made real in Jesus Christ. Our Lord picks us up again, and by the power of the Spirit we, with Christ in us, can live the Kingdom life with confidence.

REFLECTION

1. What does it mean for you to live the new, deeper life with confidence? How will you know that you are living it with confidence?

ACTION

1. "We have overcome!" How real is this knowledge and

awareness for you? What steps do you need to take to make this truth real and practical in your life? List these steps. Do them for one week. Then reflect on the week. What happened? What changed?

---

1. The following explanation about John's purpose is adapted and paraphrased from J.E. McDermond, *1, 2, 3 John*, (Harrisonburg, VA; Waterloo, ON: Herald Press, 2011) 109-110.
2. For this explanation I am indebted to McDermond, *1, 2, 3 John*, 109-110.
3. See for example Ex. 10:9; Jos. 6:21; Acts 2:17-18; 1 Tim. 5:1-2.
4. Matt Redman, "Never Once," on *10,000 Reasons*, released January 1, 2011, sixsteprecords/Sparrow Records.
5. *NLT Study Bible*, New Living Translation, 2nd ed., (Carol Stream: Tyndale House Publishers, Inc., 2008), 2008.

8

LOVE THE LORD, NOT THE WORLD

"Do not love the world or anything in the world. If anyone loves the world, love for the Father is not in them. For everything in the world—the lust of the flesh, the lust of the eyes, and the pride of life—comes not from the Father but from the world. The world and its desires pass away, but whoever does the will of God lives forever." (1 John 2:15-17)

IN THE PREVIOUS CHAPTER, we learned that we can live the new life with confidence because our sins are forgiven, we know Jesus Christ lives in us, and we have overcome. But living the new, deeper life is also about experiencing joy and contentment as we live every moment in Christ with God.

We are living in a day and age where it is all about individuality, freedom, autonomy; about finding, choosing, and making your own identity. We can call this age, the Age of the Big Me, the Age of the Selfie, the iWorld.[1] We are told to find and express our true, authentic self and to do so we must be free from any external authority, expectations, or rules that may limit us.[2] It's all about autonomy and independence, doing it my way. It's the age of the iPhone, not the wePhone.[3]

In addition, the media bombard us with promises of "the good life." Advertisements, TV shows, movies, and social media are all filled with storylines, images, and themes, which promote this philosophy of self, and self-gratification. They promise that you will be content and happy if you make money any way you can, if you buy the right car, gun, clothing, or house. In this philosophy, the more we have and the more we satisfy our desires, the happier we will be.

We are tempted to look to the material world for meaning, identity, status, power, freedom, pleasure, satisfaction, contentment, happiness, and joy. But the Bible, and experience, have taught us that this mindset falls short of its promises. Instead, it leads to self-destruction and idolatry.

1 John 2:15-17 warns us of the temptations and false promises of the world. We have received so many blessings in Christ. We must not be seduced by the temptations and desires of the world. We are called to love the Lord, not the world. We experience contentment and joy when we are in Christ. Our true identity is in Christ. We are children of God, and we cannot love the things of this world, because they will prevent us from abiding in Christ and from loving the Lord.

1. Do not love the world

"Do not love the world or anything in the world. If anyone loves the world, love for the Father is not in them." (1 John 2:15)

We have seen that love—*agape*—is unmerited, undeserved, self-giving love. It is self-sacrifice, caring about and looking out for the good of others, being willing to give up our own rights and privileges for the sake of others. This love is to prefer, be content with something, or choose one thing above another. Thus, it is an act of the will, a conscious decision, and not merely an emotional reaction or feeling.

We, as believers, are faced with a very important decision as we live as God's children in this world. On the one hand, we have the world, and on the other hand the Father. We cannot love both. There is a radical choice to be made.

The Bible uses the word "world" in both positive and negative ways. On the positive side, we are told that God created the world, and it was very good. (Gen. 3:31) God loves the world, wants to save the world, and sends Jesus as Savior into the world. (John 3:16; 4:42; 1 John 4:14) Jesus Christ is the atoning sacrifice for the world. (1 John 2:2) He is the Lamb of God who removes the sins of the world. (John 1:29) He is the Light of the world. (John 1:9; 8:12; 9:5)[4]

The word "world" also has negative meanings. It is under the control of the evil one (1 John 5:19) and under the influence of the spirit of the antichrist. (1 John 4:3-4) The world did not recognize the light that was sent to them. (John 1:10; 1 John 3:) The world hates the followers of Jesus. (John 15:18-16:4; 17:14; 1 John 3;13) The world hates Jesus. (John 7:7; 15:18,23-25)[5] The word "world" here refers to the evil systems, powers, and authorities, which are under the influence of Satan and are in rebellion against God. These are the beliefs, values, practices, and actions which oppose the values of Christ's Kingdom on earth. They are against the will of God.

Why can't we love both the world and God?

We have already seen that light and darkness cannot co-exist. God is light. When we love the world, we are in the darkness, and we cannot have fellowship with God. James 4:4 says, "...don't you know that friendship with the world means enmity against God? Therefore, anyone who chooses to be a friend of the world becomes an enemy of God."

We are dead to the world, and the world is dead to us because through the cross of our Lord the world has been crucified to us, and we to the world. (Gal 6:14) We have died to the world and to self. The old way of life is dead to us, and the world no longer matters to us. We are part of a better world, a better system—the kingdom of God. We have a new, eternal life that is far better than this world.

Jesus also said, "No one can serve two masters. Either you will hate the one and love the other, or you will be devoted to the one and despise the other. You cannot serve both God and money." (Matt. 6:24)

There is a love decision to be made. We cannot love God and the world. This does not mean that we should hate the world, life, or being human. Not everything in the world is bad, evil, or sinful. The good world, the created order, is there as an instrument to worship God, serve his Kingdom, and serve others. We are not to exploit the world for selfish purposes or worship the creation but the Creator.

The world becomes a problem when we are consumed by the things of the world, when the values of human society—culture, economics, and politics—define and shape us. Instead, we should be shaped by Jesus' values—kingdom values. Our passion should not be for what culture, politics, the economy, or material things offer, but for what God desires.

I believe that too many Christians are trying to sit on the fence between God and the world. When it suits them, they will speak out against sin and injustices in the world. But when it does not suit them, for whatever reason, they ignore it. They remain silent and do not take action against sin or injustice. They live by double standards. Christianity has a bad reputation because of this hypocrisy. We see this happening especially in social media. It seems that Christians think they can stop being Christian when they are on social media and not dealing with someone face-to-face. They insult others, speak out in anger, use hate language, do not love and respect others.

We must live the Jesus-life all the time and everywhere. Wherever we are—at home, in the workplace, in school, on the sports field, or on the Internet, we must live the Jesus-life. We should love others, including our enemies, even on Facebook, Instagram, and Twitter. We cannot participate in name calling or post things that demean others. We must maintain our integrity as God's people so that our witness to Jesus Christ will be credible. Only when we live the Jesus-life with integrity, deal honestly with sin and injustices in our own lives, and love others, can we speak out against the sin and injustices in the world.

There is a war waging between the world's evil desires and God's desires, between what people want and what God wants. The things of this world are not from the Father. Love for the world's ways and the world's things squeezes out love for God.[6] It Edges God Out: E.G.O.[7] Our ego replaces God.

2. THE THINGS OF THE WORLD

What are the things of the world? How do people love the world? John sums up love for the world into three categories: the lust of the flesh, the lust of the eyes, and the pride of life. All three categories show selfishness, self-centeredness, and self-gratification. All three are attitudes of the heart. Jesus said in Luke 6:45, "an evil man brings evil things out of the evil stored up in his heart. For the mouth speaks what the heart is full of." We could also say that the hand does what the heart is full of.

2.1 THE LUST OF THE FLESH.

These are the desires or cravings of our old sinful self. The focus is on self-gratification—"wanting my own way." It is when we are obsessed or preoccupied with satisfying our physical desires that they lead to gluttony, drunkenness, sexual immorality, materialism, envy, jealousy, hatred, fits of rage, and so on.[8] These cravings of the flesh prevent us from thinking clearly, biblically, and Christianly, because we follow the desires of our ego. The argument in favor of these desires is, "It cannot be wrong, because it feels so good; it must be from God." We lose common sense. When we do this, we give ourselves over to the deeds of darkness. Paul says, "Rather, clothe yourselves with the Lord Jesus Christ, and do not think about how to gratify the desires of the flesh." (Rom 13:14)

2.2 THE LUST OF THE EYES.

The eyes are the windows to our souls, to our hearts. But they are also the entry points for evil into our hearts. (Matt. 5:28; 6:22-23)[9] The desire of the eyes is the craving for everything we see—wanting everything for ourselves. It causes us to covet and want more. We are never content with what we have. Enough is never enough. We bow to the idol of materialism.[10] And this leads to comparison, envy, jealousy, and competition, which pushes out love for others, in order to make a place for the love of self alone.

For example, I have a perfectly good hunting rifle. It works fine, is accurate, and I have hunted successfully with it. I do not need anything better. However, the other day, I went hunting with my friend, and I saw his new rifle. It is beautiful and has more and better features than mine. As I looked at it, I compared and became envious. I was no longer content with what I had and wanted to have a rifle like his. So, I went and bought one. Next year, a newer model comes out; I'll see it, want it . . . You know where this story goes.

We cannot always avoid what we see with our eyes, but what do we do with what we see? Will we allow our eyes to cause us to stumble? Or will we clothe ourselves with Jesus, abide in Christ, capture every thought for Jesus, and think about kingdom things?

2.3 THE PRIDE OF LIFE.

This category refers to the arrogant boasting and taking pride in our worldly possessions and earthly achievements. We strive to accumulate wealth. We strive to achieve positions of power. We are obsessed with our status and importance. The pride of life refers to persons who are doing all of this without seeking God's will, without trusting God. They take pride in themselves, in what they have and who they have become. Listen to James 4:13-17:

Now listen, you who say, 'Today or tomorrow we will go to this or that city, spend a year there, carry on business and make money.' Why, you do not even know what will happen tomorrow. What is your life? You are a mist that appears for a little while and then vanishes. Instead, you ought to say, 'If it is the Lord's will, we will live and do this or that.' As it is, you boast in your arrogant schemes. All such boasting is evil. If anyone, then, knows the good they ought to do and doesn't do it, it is sin for them.

"Those who trust in their riches will fall" (Prov. 11:28), and those "who trust in themselves are fools" (Prov. 28:26). "In their hearts, humans plan their course, but the Lord establishes their steps." (Prov. 16:9)

When God blesses you with wealth, success, and positions of power and leadership, these do not belong to you, and they are not for you. God has blessed you with these so that you can care for others, bless others, help others, and love others in action. (1 John 3:16-18; Rev. 3:17; Prov. 11:24-26) You are to use these to serve God's Kingdom, to worship, glorify, and exalt God only. "Commit to the Lord whatever you do and he will establish your plans." (Prov. 16:3) "Do not wear yourself out to get rich; do not trust your own cleverness. Cast but a glance at riches, and they are gone, for they will surely sprout wings and fly off to the sky like an eagle." (Prov. 23:4-5).

The world and its things tempt us with all kinds of promises, but they do not deliver the "good life" and the freedom they promise.

Instead, they enslave you. They do not give happiness, except for a superficial joy that lasts for a short while and then disappears. We are never content, always wanting more. And so we become entangled and imprisoned. We are consumed with worry. How will I get it; how will I get more; how will I achieve more? And once I have it, I worry, "How will I maintain it?" We are then controlled by the values and viewpoints of the world and not the Kingdom. They edge God out, and they become our idols—our new gods.

We are also consumed with our identity.

"I have to work hard to make my name, to establish my identity. Will people accept me, like me, love me?"

We forget that we already have a clear identity in Christ. We are children of the living God. We are fully accepted. We are loved unconditionally and totally. We are no longer slaves to sin. We are no longer slaves to our desires. We are no longer slaves to fear or worry. "Do not worry about any of these things. Seek first the kingdom, and his righteousness, and all these things will be given to you as well." (Matt. 6:33) We have been set free and are now the "slaves to righteousness." (Rom. 6:18-19)

3. THEY ARE ALL PASSING AWAY

We should not love the world because it and its desires are passing away. Jesus said, "Do not store up for yourselves treasures on earth, where moths and vermin destroy, and where thieves break in and steal." (Matt. 6:19) Remember the parable of the rich fool in Luke 12:16-21 who was blessed with abundance, planned to build barns, and then "God said to him, 'You fool! This very night your life will be demanded from you. Then who will get what you have prepared for yourself?' This is how it will be with whoever stores up things for themselves but is not rich toward God."

James 5:1-6 teaches us:

Now listen, you rich people, weep and wail because of the misery that is coming on you. Your wealth has rotted, and moths have eaten your clothes. Your gold and silver are corroded. Their corrosion will testify against you and eat your flesh like fire. You have hoarded wealth in the last days. Look! The wages you failed to pay the workers who mowed your fields are crying out against you. The cries of the harvesters have reached the ears of the Lord Almighty. You have lived on earth in luxury and self-indulgence. You have fattened yourselves in the day of slaugh-

ter. *You have condemned and murdered the innocent one, who was not opposing you.*

This present age with its oppressive systems, this world ruled and influenced by the evil one, is all coming to an end. All material things come to an end. Life, physical life as we know it, comes to an end. And when it comes to an end, where will we be?

Someone said, "To give in to the senseless lust for possessions and power, to spend money on selfish desires and foolish upgrades in cars, clothes, homes, and equipment while ignoring the needs of others is to lose the cosmic war to Satan."[11] I would like to add that it is to lose the battle of our souls to Satan. And it is not worth it. You may gain everything you want in this life, but you will lose your soul. (Mark 8:35-36; Matt. 10:28) And when everything passes away, you enter eternal death, not eternal life.

All is passing away because, in Jesus Christ, God's kingdom has come. It is moving toward its fulfillment when everything will be united under Christ's rule, and there will be a new heaven and a new earth. Knowing that this world will end, knowing that God's Kingdom is here and coming, gives us hope and the courage to deny ourselves the temporary pleasures in this world in order to enjoy what God has promised for eternity.[12] This gives us the courage to love the Lord and live the new, eternal life, now and forever.

4. Love the Lord and live the eternal life!

We love the Lord and live the new life by doing the will of God. "Do not conform to the pattern of this world, but be transformed by the renewing of your mind. Then you will be able to test and approve what God's will is—his good, pleasing and perfect will." (Rom. 12:2)

Ephesians 5:10,15,18 says, "Find out what pleases the Lord . . . Be very careful how you live—not as unwise but as wise—making the most of every opportunity, because the days are evil. Therefore do not be foolish, but understand what the Lord's will is . . . be filled with the Holy Spirit."

And that is how we can do the will of God and live the new, eternal life—by the power of the Holy Spirit and putting on the full armor of God. (Eph. 6:11)

What do we value? What do we treasure? The world or the kingdom? Ourselves or the Lord?

We do not need to seek our identity, joy, contentment, happiness, or meaning in the things of the world because we are already in Christ. We have a new mindset, a new worldview: "Since, then, you have been raised with Christ, set your hearts on things above, where Christ is, seated at the right hand of God. Set your minds on things above, not on earthly things. For you died, and your life is now hidden with Christ in God. When Christ, who is your life, appears, then you also will appear with him in glory." (Col. 3:1-4).

So, what should we do?

Abide in Christ every moment.

When you begin your day, begin it with Jesus. Don't ask, "What will I do today?" But ask, "Jesus, what would we do? What do you want me to do?"

When confronted with decisions, don't ask, "What should I do?" Ask, "Lord, what would *we* do? What are you trying to teach me in this situation?"

Talk with Christ about what you see, what you hear and read about what is happening, and what you are afraid of. This is much better than asking the question, "What would Jesus do?" That question keeps Jesus outside of you. But Christ is living in us, and we are in him, and when we are talking with him that union becomes real.[13]

We do not need to seek our identity, joy, contentment, and meaning in the things of the world because we are already in Christ, and our life is hidden with Christ in God. Our life is in God's hands. We are children of God with a new life in Christ.

Therefore, we experience contentment and joy in this life as we live for and love the Lord and others.

REFLECTION

1. What are the things of the world that you still love, that you have a hard time not loving? Identify these, and bring them to the Lord in prayer.

ACTION

Try to do the following for at least a week. Don't stop after a week. Reflect on what happened during the week, and then continue to do this every day.
1. Begin your day with the question, "Lord, what would we do today?"
2. When faced with decisions, stop, become silent, even if only for a minute. Center your focus on Jesus, become aware of his presence, and then ask him, "What would we do, Jesus?"

---

1. See Rankin Wilbourne, *Union with Christ: The Way to Know and Enjoy God* (Colorado Springs, CO: David C Cook, 2016), Kindle loc 1640-43, referring to David Brooks, *The Road to Character*, (New York: Random, 2015), Kindle loc 244, & Dale S. Kuehne, *Sex and the iWorld: Rethinking Relationship Beyond an Age of Individualism*, (Grand Rapids, MI: Baker Academic, 2009), 32.
2. See Wilbourne, *Union*, Kindle loc 1632-1652.
3. Wilbourne, Kindle loc 1658.
4. J.E. McDermond, *1, 2, 3 John*, (Harrisonburg, VA; Waterloo, ON: Herald Press, 2011), 129.
5. McDermond, *1, 2, 3 John*, 129.
6. Eugene Peterson, *The Message: The Bible in contemporary language*, (Colorado Springs, CO: NavPress, 2005).
7. Ken Blanchard, Phil Hodges, Lee Ross, & Avery Willis, *Lead Like Jesus: Beginning the Journey*, (Nashville: J. Countryman, 2003), 30.
8. See the lists in Galatians 5:19-21; Ephesians 5:3-7; and Colossians 3:5-9. See also 1 Corinthians 6:18.
9. McDermond, 131.

10. Bruce B. Barton & Grant R. Osborne, *1, 2 & 3 John*, Life Application Bible Commentary (Wheaton, IL: Tyndale House, 1998), 45
11. Barton & Osborne, *1, 2 & 3 John*, 43.
12. *NIV Life Application Study Bible*, (Grand Rapids, MI: Zondervan, 2011), 2118.
13. See Wilbourne, Kindle loc 1808-1818, for his discussion on reframing the conversation from "What Would Jesus Do?" to talking with Christ about what we should do.

9
REMAIN IN CHRIST

"Dear children, this is the last hour; and as you have heard that the antichrist is coming, even now many antichrists have come. This is how we know it is the last hour. They went out from us, but they did not really belong to us. For if they had belonged to us, they would have remained with us; but their going showed that none of them belonged to us.

"But you have an anointing from the Holy One, and all of you know the truth. I do not write to you because you do not know the truth, but because you do know it and because no lie comes from the truth. Who is the liar? It is whoever denies that Jesus is the Christ. Such a person is the antichrist—denying the Father and the Son. No one who denies the Son has the Father; whoever acknowledges the Son has the Father also.

"As for you, see that what you have heard from the beginning remains in you. If it does, you also will remain in the Son and in the Father. And this is what he promised us—eternal life.

"I am writing these things to you about those who are trying to lead you astray. As for you, the anointing you received from him remains in you, and you do not need anyone to teach you. But as his anointing teaches you about all things and as that anointing is real, not counterfeit —just as it has taught you, remain in him." (1 John 2:18-27)

1. This is the Last Hour!

WE, like the believers in John's time, are living in the last hour, the end times. This is the time between Jesus' first coming and his second coming. These are the last days.

Our Lord Jesus Christ warned us that during these times, false messiahs, false Christs, and false prophets will appear to deceive the world and lead believers astray. (Mark 13:21-22; Matt. 24:4-5,24) Paul warns us, "Savage wolves will come in among you and will not spare the flock. Even from your own number men will arise and distort the truth in order to draw away disciples after them." (Acts 20:29-30)

This happened in John's churches. Antichrists divided the church, left the church, and tried to lead the believers astray. These antichrists are the forerunners of the one Antichrist[1] that will come just before Christ's second coming as we are told in 2 Thessalonians 2:3-10 and Revelation 13. These antichrists are real, and they are also active today. Who are they?

An antichrist is anyone who denies that Jesus is the Christ, the Messiah, the Savior, the Son of God. And to deny Jesus is to deny God's way of revealing himself to the world. It is denying God's way of saving the world. Antichrists are opposed to God, to God's mission, and God's kingdom.

When we deny Jesus, we are not in Christ, and Christ is not in us. Then we cannot remain in Christ. And when we are not in Christ, we cannot know and have fellowship with the Father. Jesus is the only way to know and have fellowship with the Father. And to know the Father is to have eternal life. (John 14 and 17)

We should not be deceived and led astray by other religions or new age spiritualities that say there are other ways to know and have fellowship with God. Only Jesus is the Life, the Way, and the Truth.

Today there are many antichrists active in the world. They are the atheists who completely deny the existence of God. They are the people who deny Jesus, saying that he is a mythical figure. They are the people who recognize Jesus as a historical figure, but not as the Messiah, the Son of God. According to them he lived and died, but was not resurrected. Then there are those false messiahs and false prophets, who pretend to be Christians, but deceive people with false teachings and lead them astray into all kinds of cults.[2]

We talked about how God's kingdom and his people, the church, and followers of Jesus are being attacked, vilified, and mocked from all sides. Moral standards are being broken down all around us. The predominant value in our society and culture seems to be "Do whatever pleases you. Look out for self. Gratify yourself." There is no or very little consideration for others, their rights, their freedoms, their human worth, value, and dignity.

We are living in a day and age where people are desperate for meaning, purpose, and truth. For some time now, the postmodern worldview about truth has shaped culture and society. That is, "What is true for you is the truth, what works for you is good and true, what feels good is right and true."

However, we are now discovering that this philosophy is not working. It is not fulfilling its promises of freedom and fulfillment. Society is falling apart. What is good? What is bad? What is true? People are desperately seeking for the truth.

In times like these, even believers begin to doubt. Is our faith true? Is Jesus real? Is following Jesus the right path? Is living the kingdom life really worthwhile? Is the church necessary? Is it not an old-fashioned habit, an antiquated institution with no relevance today?

It is easy for believers to become discouraged, anxious, and fearful. John encourages and reassures us that we do not need to fear these antichrists. There is no need for us to listen to false, misleading teachings. There is no need for us to doubt the truth. Why?

2. We are filled with the Holy Spirit

We do not need to doubt because we are filled with the Holy Spirit. We have an anointing from the Holy One. When we believed, we were filled with the Holy Spirit (1 Cor. 12:13). The Spirit of truth guides us into all the truth. The Spirit teaches us all things and reminds us of everything Jesus has taught us. (John 14:26; 16:13)

Because the Spirit teaches us about all things, we know the truth and we do not need other teachers, teachings, or claims of truth. No lies, falsehoods, or deceptions can come from the Holy Spirit. The Holy Spirit is truth. The Holy Spirit is real and living in us. (1 John 2:27).

Therefore, we can experience the new, deeper life, but we must walk in step with the Spirit. How do we do this?

We must ensure that what we have heard from the beginning remains in us. (1 John 2:24) Verse 27 repeats: "Remain in him."

3. Remain in Jesus Christ—Keeping in step with the Spirit

We must remain, abide, and live deeply in Christ. The following ideas and illustrations on how to abide in Christ are borrowed from Wilbourne's book, *Union with Christ: The Way to Know and Enjoy God*.[3]

But first, there is a very important question we must answer honestly. Do you really want to live the new, deeper life with God? Do you really want to know God? Do you really want to fall in love with God more?

If God is not the end of your desire and the purpose of your life, then these calls to abide in Christ will become mere obligations and duties to perform. They will be an increased burden laid on a heavy load you are already carrying.

Is God your true God? Is God really the one your heart is after? You may profess faith in God, you may claim that you believe, while you are actually attempting to use him as a means to your own ends. "Whatever your heart seeks most—that is your real god."[4]

Is your prayer, "I want to know Christ?" (Phil. 3:10)

If yes, then let's begin this journey of abiding in Christ.

4. Our union with Christ—Christ in us, we in Christ

Why is it so important to remain and abide in Christ?

Because of our union with Christ.[5] Our union with Christ is the central reality of our salvation. It is central to the Bible's story. It is central to First John. Who we are and what we are becoming flows out of our union with Christ. At the center of God's mission stands Jesus Christ. Jesus united his life to ours, and so brought us back into the presence of God the Father. (Eph 2:18; 1 Pet 3:18)

Our union with Christ gives us the amazing gift of eternal life, living forever in the presence of God. But this life begins now. Our citizenship is in heaven (Phil 3:20), but we are God's children now. (1 John 3:2) And to live as children of God here and now, we must keep on abiding in Christ to become perfect like Christ, so that when he comes, we will be ready—righteous, pure, confident, and unashamed before him. Abiding in Christ is how we live out our union with Christ.

So what is union with Christ? Union with Christ means that we are in Christ, and Christ is in us.[6]

4.1 We are in Christ

Christ represents all of us who believe in Jesus as the Son of God. When we are united to Christ, we share in all that he has done for us. We have been "crucified with Christ" (Gal. 2:20), "buried ... with him." (Rom. 6:4) We died with him. We were "raised with Christ." (Col. 3:1) "I no longer live, but Christ lives in me." (Gal 2:20) "If anyone is in Christ, he is a new creation." (2 Cor 5:17) We are even "seated . . . with him in the heavenly places." (Eph. 2: 6)[7] This is all possible because Jesus, the Son of God, became fully human like us.[8]

And "the life I now live in the body I live by faith in the Son of God who loved me and gave himself for me."[9] Yes, we are still living in these earthly bodies, but we have been changed fundamentally and radically. This change is so radical that Jesus calls it a new birth—we are born again through the Holy Spirit.(John 3:5-8)

This union becomes active, real, and powerful in our lives because of faith. Jesus represents us before the Father. We are completely safe, hidden in Christ. When we, as sinners, enter into God's presence, his holiness and righteousness, will zap us like a bug zapper because sin cannot be in his presence. But Christ's holiness, righteousness, and purity covers us and makes us holy, pure, and righteous. When God looks at us, he sees us hidden in Christ. He sees our holiness and righteousness that comes from Christ. Therefore, we can now enter freely and without fear into his presence. As Wilbourne says, "This is freedom. This is confidence. This is good, good news."[10]

4.2 Christ is in us

In John 14:16-18 Jesus said, "I will ask the Father, and he will give you another advocate to help you and be with you forever—the Spirit of truth. The world cannot accept him, because it neither sees him nor knows him. But you know him, for he lives with you and will be in you. I will not leave you as orphans; I will come to you."

The Father will give us another advocate—helper, comforter, counselor—another who is like Jesus, and he is the Holy Spirit of truth. We have Jesus within us (Col. 1:17), wherever we are and wherever we go. This is why Jesus could say in Matthew 28:20, "I am with you always." Jesus now dwells in us by his Spirit.

To be united with Christ is to have the Spirit of Christ within us. The incarnate, crucified, resurrected and exalted Christ is living in us. His power and life enter into our lives to transform us, not only to atone for our sinful past, but also to liberate us now, and empower us to live a radically new life.[11]

Through Christ, by the Holy Spirit, we have a personal, vital, and real relationship with God. Union with Christ is not just an idea to be understood, but a new reality to be lived through faith. "We are already completely clothed in Christ and his righteousness, but life in Christ is one of growing up into this new reality until it fits us. We are not striving to attain it. We are striving to lay hold of what is already ours. We are growing up into it."[12]

What is this new reality?

5. We are Children of God

Because of our union with Christ, we are children of God. "To all who did receive him, to those who believed in his name, he gave the right to become children of God." (John 1:12) "So in Christ Jesus, you are all children of God through faith, for all of you who were baptized into Christ have clothed yourselves with Christ." (Gal. 2:26) "God sent his Son . . . that we might receive adoption to sonship. Because you are his sons, God sent the Spirit of his Son into our hearts, the Spirit who calls out, 'Abba, Father.' So you are no longer a slave, but God's child; and since you are his child, God has made you also an heir." (Gal. 4:5-7).

We are children of God. And that is what we are (1 John 3:1-2). This is not just a title, but a reality. God does not just call us children, he makes us exactly that: his children.[13] We are God's children—now![14]

We are growing up into Christlikeness. We are being perfected. We do not know what we will be, how this will look, because the full glory of Christ has not yet been revealed (1 John 3:2). But we do know when Christ comes back, we will be like him. When he is revealed, we will see him and know him in his full glory, and we will be like him. (1 John 3:3) We will be perfect as he is perfect.

God is at work in us, changing us. This gives us tremendous hope, courage, and confidence as we struggle to overcome our old self and to live the new life in this world. We live this new life by abiding in Christ. In the next two chapters, we continue to explore how to abide and keep on abiding in Christ.

REFLECTION

1. Take some time to meditate on the reality that you are a child of God, a son or daughter of God.

- What does this fact that you are a child of God mean for you?
- How does this make you feel?
- How will this change the way you view yourself and life? How will this change how you do things?

ACTION

Whenever you doubt yourself, experience fear or anxiety, whenever someone rejects you or look down upon you, stop, become quiet, and meditate on the truth that you are a child of God. Let that reality flow into your whole being. Let that reality comfort, encourage, and guide you in your next steps as you continue to live the new life in Christ.

---

1. Bruce B. Barton and Grant R. Osborne, *1, 2 & 3 John*, Life Application Bible Commentary (Wheaton, IL: Tyndale House, 1998), 48.
2. The term cult is theologically "used of those systems that profess to be Christian but that are antagonistic to the basic doctrines of Scripture ... Inherent in cult worship is the elevation of some authority to or beyond an equality with the Biblical revelation ... a cult is, in effect, idolatry posing as Christianity, for whatever protestations are made to the contrary, worship

based on a repudiation of fundamental Bible truth is idolatry" — Alan Cairns, *Dictionary of Theological Terms* (Belfast; Greenville, SC: Ambassador Emerald International, 2002), 120–121.
3. See Rankin Wilbourne, *Union with Christ: The Way to Know and Enjoy God* (Colorado Springs, CO: David C Cook, 2016), especially chapter 11.
4. Wilbourne, *Union*, Kindle loc 2622-2624.
5. For this section on our union with Christ I give full credit to Wilbourne, *Union with Christ*, especially ch. 2 , Kindle loc 422-658. This section is based on and follow the ideas, thinking, and outline of Wilbourne's book.
6. Wilbourne, *Union*, Kindle loc 439-456.
7. Wilbourne, Kindle loc 469-472.
8. Wilbourne, Kindle loc 476-480.
9. Wilbourne, Kindle loc 495-412.
10. Wilbourne, Kindle loc 514-515.
11. Wilbourne, Kindle loc 549-566.
12. Wilbourne, Kindle loc 655-657.
13. See Bruce B. Barton & Grant R. Osborne, *1, 2 & 3 John*, Life Application Bible Commentary (Wheaton, IL: Tyndale House, 1998), 62.
14. Barton & Osborne, *1, 2 & 3 John*, 62.

10
SAILING WITH CHRIST

"As for you, see that what you have heard from the beginning remains in you. If it does, you also will remain in the Son and in the Father. And this is what he promised us—eternal life.

"I am writing these things to you about those who are trying to lead you astray. As for you, the anointing you received from him remains in you, and you do not need anyone to teach you. But as his anointing teaches you about all things and as that anointing is real, not counterfeit —just as it has taught you, remain in him." (1 John 2:24-27)

WE ARE CHILDREN OF GOD. We live as God's children when we abide in Christ and walk in step with the Holy Spirit. How do we remain in Jesus Christ? How do we live in the power of the Spirit?

Have you sailed a boat, gone windsurfing or kitesurfing? These have two things in common. They need the wind as well as sails to catch the wind. You cannot control the wind, its direction, strength, or speed. But you can set your sails so that you can catch the wind and move forward. For this, you need to learn the skills and use those skills to set the sails to catch the power and energy of the wind.

It is the same with abiding in Christ. Christ lives in us. He came and took up residence in our hearts. We are filled with the Holy Spirit. It is a gift of grace from God. We cannot control any of these. We cannot control the power, the wind, of the Holy Spirit. (John 3:8) But we can learn to set and manage the sails of our lives and souls so that we can live by the power of the Spirit. That is what abiding in Christ is all about.

There are two very important steps needed to set our sails to catch the power of the Spirit and to remain in Christ. Living in Christ is described in the Bible as walking with Christ, keeping in step with the Holy Spirit.[1] These steps are: *faith* and *repentance*.[2]

"The first step in our life with God is always the step of faith."[3] "Now faith is confidence in what we hope for and assurance about what we do not see." (Heb. 11:1) Faith is being able to say, "This I know, come what may, that God is God. He is alive, and He loves me. I am forgiven, I am saved, I am a child of God. I have new, eternal life."

If we are not sure that we have been saved, if we are not certain that God loves us, we will not seek God's face, but rather try to flee from him. We believe in Jesus Christ as Lord and Savior. We believe that He is alive and living in us. We believe.

The next step is repentance. "Repentance is not simply feeling sorry for what we've done or confessing where we've failed. Nor is it simply resolving to do better. Rather, repentance is turning back to God in all of life. If sin is running from God to get control of our lives, then repentance is turning back to God and yielding control to him."[4]

Wilbourne explains that we keep in step with the Spirit through ". . . faith and repentance. Believe and obey. These are the left, right, left, right of our walk with God. Every day we step out in faith." And every day we turn back to God and real life with repentance.[5]

The Christian life is like a bicycle.[6] To move forward it must have two wheels. The front wheel is grace. Grace always leads. It comes first. The back wheel is demand—God's will. Obedience always follows grace.

Belief and repentance are like the pedals. We must keep pressing on both to move forward. Have you tried riding a bicycle with only one pedal? It's very hard to make progress.

It is all grace. By God's grace, his Holy Spirit created faith in our hearts to believe. By grace, God sent his Son. By grace, we are saved through faith in Jesus Christ. By grace and the work of the Holy Spirit we repent. In faith, we receive God's gift of salvation, the forgiveness of sin and new, eternal life.

Then, because we have experienced this amazing grace, we obey Jesus as our Lord. We want to live the new life we have in Christ. Out of reverence for Christ (Eph. 5:21), because we worship him as Lord, we do his will.

Faith and repentance are like spiritual breathing.[7] We breathe in the promises of God. We believe. We breathe out the lies and sins of trying to abide in things other than Christ. We repent. Like regular breathing, this spiritual breathing is repetitive, continuous, and absolutely essential for the life in Christ.

The more you believe the gospel, the more you will repent. The more you obey God, the more you will believe God. And the more you believe God, the more you will want to obey him.[8] The more you remain in Christ, the more you will fall in love with God, delight in and enjoy the Lord, and live the deeper life.

The wind of God's love, grace, and power is never ceasing. And every day, remaining in Christ enables us to catch this wind. It is our union with Christ that keeps us from drifting away. And the power of the Spirit, the wind in our sails, keeps us moving forward. "We must pay the most careful attention, therefore, to what we have heard, so that we do not drift away." (Heb. 2:1)

The only way is to sail with Christ, to remain in Christ, to keep on abiding in Christ. Jesus said in John 15:5, "apart from me you can do nothing."

In the next chapter, we will learn some of the skills for

setting our sails to catch the power of the Spirit and sail with Christ.

REFLECTION & ACTION

I AM IN CHRIST. CHRIST IS IN ME.

Try this exercise[9] every morning when you get up.

While using the mirror for your morning rituals, pause for a while and look yourself deep in the eyes in the mirror. *What* do you see? *Who* do you see? Yourself?

Yes, but there is more. Jesus Christ is in you. The eyes and face looking back at you are not only you but also Christ in you. Reflect on this while you are looking yourself in the eyes. Take a few minutes to ponder the fact that looking back at you is both Jesus and yourself. Imagine his eyes, his face overlaying your own. Be aware of his presence in you. Declare to yourself, "Christ is in me. I am in Christ." See him. Feel him.

Do this every morning for at least a week and see what happens. After experiencing this for a week, imagine doing it for the rest of your life. This little practical discipline every morning will launch you on a journey of abiding in Christ—of beginning to live every moment with him. Begin the day with him! The more you do this, the more he will be with you, in you, and you in him during the day.

1. Commit yourself to do the exercise described above. Do this exercise every morning or evening for one week.

2. After one week take some time to reflect on the past week and the exercise. How did you experience the exercise? What were your feelings? What were your thoughts? What have you learned? What changes have you noticed in your life? How has your relationship with God and your abiding in Christ changed?
[10]

1. Wilbourne, Kindle loc 2632-2648.
2. See Wilbourne, Kindle loc 2651 & 2670.
3. Wilbourne, Kindle loc 2650.
4. Wilbourne, Kindle loc 2672-2674.
5. Wilbourne Kindle loc 2679-2682.
6. This illustration is borrowed from Wilbourne, *Union*, chapter 11.
7. Wilbourne Kindle loc 2680-2698.
8. Wilbourne, Kindle loc 2700-2703.
9. The idea for this exercise adapted from a similar exercise in Gary W. Moon, *Apprenticeship with Jesus: Learning to Live Like the Master*, (Grand Rapids, MI: Baker Books, 2009), 64.
10. This illustration of sailing borrowed from Rankin Wilbourne, *Union with Christ: The Way to Know and Enjoy God* (Colorado Springs, CO: David C Cook, 2016), chapter 11.

11
KEEP ON ABIDING IN CHRIST

"And now, dear children, continue in him, so that when he appears we may be confident and unashamed before him at his coming. If you know that he is righteous, you know that everyone who does what is right has been born of him. See what great love the Father has lavished on us, that we should be called children of God! And that is what we are! The reason the world does not know us is that it did not know him. Dear friends, now we are children of God, and what we will have not yet been made known. But we know that when Christ appears, we shall be like him, for we shall see him as he is. All who have this hope in him purify themselves, just as he is pure." (1 John 2:28-3:3)

WE HAVE LEARNED that to abide in Christ, we must set the sails of our souls to catch the wind, the power of the Holy Spirit. We talked about the first steps we need to take to set our sails, namely faith and repentance. Now let's explore the practical skills for setting our sails.

1. SET YOUR SAILS TO CATCH THE POWER OF THE SPIRIT[1]

God gave us the spiritual disciplines to train our souls. These are our means of abiding in Christ. These are the skills to set our sails.

Richard Foster defines spiritual disciplines this way: "God has given us the disciplines of the spiritual life as a means of receiving his grace. The disciplines allow us to place ourselves before God so that he can transform us."[2]

They are essential for abiding in Christ, but these disciplines do not change us. God changes us. The spiritual disciplines just help us to yield to the power of the Spirit. "They are ordinary means God has provided for us to experience his extraordinary grace."[3]

These disciplines put us in a place where God can work within us. And our union with Christ changes how we view and do these spiritual disciplines. They are no longer mechanical duties that we are obliged to do because it is the Christian thing to do. They are opportunities to come into the presence of the living Christ.[4] We want to do them. We look forward to them with expectation and joy.

Let us review some of the spiritual disciplines[5] that enable us to set our sails so that they will be filled with God's powerful wind.

2. Remain in God's Word

We abide in Christ by the *daily meditation on God's Word*. How do you approach your reading and study of the Bible? As something to get over quickly so that you can go on with the next thing in your life? Or do "you approach the Bible with the expectation that the same Spirit who inspired these words long ago, is the same Spirit who is in you now, speaking to you"[6] and teaching you?

The Bible is "living and active" (Heb. 4: 12), because the living Christ, who is dwelling in us, is actively speaking through it. Through the Holy Spirit and by prayer we meditate on the Word until it gets into our bloodstream and becomes an integral part of our life. The Bible is not just a "toolbox for navigating life's problems." First and foremost, it is one of the means God provided for us to experience his presence—for us to have fellowship with him. And then out of that fellowship, we navigate life's journey.[7] When we remain and abide in his Word, we remain and abide in Christ. And the more and deeper we are in his presence, the more we will become like him.

3. Persist in Prayer

We abide in Christ by *persisting in prayer*. "Does prayer make a difference? Won't God do what God will do? . . . Why should we have to keep asking God for what he already knows we need?" The question is rather, "Do we know what we need?"[8]

"We often don't know what is best for us," but God knows. So the call to persist in prayer is for our sake, not God's. "'The LORD is near to all who call on him' (Ps. 145:18), but for us to know God is near—nearer to us than we can imagine—we must call out to him."[9] Our Father desires to hear from us, his children. And he always hears our prayers. Kierkegaard said, "This is our comfort because God answers every prayer, for either he gives what we pray for or something far better."[10]

Prayer is integral—essential—to abiding in Christ because prayer is about having a personal, intimate conversation with God. Prayer is not only asking things from God but also expressing our adoration for God, praising him and giving thanks to him. Prayer is also about silence. We need to be silent in God's presence to listen and hear his voice. Prayer is fellowship with God, made possible by our union with Christ. (Heb. 4:16)[11]

4. Worship

We abide in Christ by *worshipping together*. "Union with Christ changes how we worship."[12] We do not come to church to evaluate the music or the quality of the sermon. We come into worship expecting to hear from God. "Christ is our high priest who is leading us into his Father's presence (Heb. 8:1-2), and that Christ is speaking to us through all the elements of the worship service." So instead of observing passively, ask yourself actively during every worship service, "God, what do you want to do in me now? What do you want me to hear? How do you want my life to look different as a result of being here?"[13]

Because our faith is weak, God gave us symbols to remind us of the gospel. These are the sacraments (or ordinances), baptism and the Lord's Supper. They are "visible signs of an invisible reality," visible forms of God's invisible grace. Baptism is a sign of our union with Christ. The Lord's Supper is a sign of our ongoing union with Christ. When we participate in the Lord's Supper, we have fellowship with the living Christ and his body. "Is not the cup of thanksgiving for which we give thanks a participation in the blood of Christ? And is not the bread that we break a participation in the body of Christ?" (1 Cor. 10:16)[14]

5. Fellowship

We abide in Christ by *having fellowship with one another*. Union with Christ also means being united to all the other believers who are in Him. Abiding in Christ cannot be separated from abiding in the Christian community, in the Church.[15] The Christian life was never meant to be lived alone. "We were made for community. How could it be otherwise when we are created in the image of a God who is himself a community of three persons?"[16] Bonhoeffer said, "The Christian needs another Christian who speaks God's word to him . . . again and again when he becomes uncertain and discouraged."[17]

We so easily doubt the promises of the gospel. We so easily disobey and sin. We need a community in which to confess our sins to one another (James 5:16). We need community to hear the gospel spoken over our lives by others. On this journey, we need to "help one another, spur one another on, and carry one another's burdens . . . we need spiritual friends. We need friends to help us see our blind spots. On our own, it can be easy to deceive ourselves. But encourage one another daily, as long as it is called Today, so that none of you may be hardened by sin's deceitfulness." (Heb. 3: 13).[18]

6. WHAT ABOUT THE DOLDRUMS?[19]

Sailors experience what is called doldrums. The wind is quiet. No matter how you set your sails, there is no wind to catch. Your ship is dead in the water. In the same way, we will experience the doldrums in our spiritual lives. There will be times when you set your sails and nothing happens. "You are doing everything right. You are reading the living Word, but it does not seem alive. You are praying to the living God, but it seems like no one's listening. You are worshipping, but it just sounds like noise. You're doing all you know how to do, yet you are stuck."[20]

The doldrums happen because we are "doing the right thing for the wrong reasons." We have lost the perspective of our union in Christ.[21] You are no longer seeing these exercises as a means of abiding in Christ, as a means of living in the presence of God. You see them only as duties to perform. You see them like the wind, the end goal, and not the ways to set your sails to catch the wind. You are trying to blow wind into your sails. You are trying to control the wind. And so they become a burden, and nothing happens.

Something else can also happen. You have mastered the skills. You are setting the sails perfectly and catching the wind. You are sailing along at high speed. You are ecstatic, enjoying every moment of the ride. You are on a spiritual high. But then pride begins to take over. You begin to think that you are in control. Pride says, "I am so good at abiding in Christ. Look at how I am growing."

And then you hit a doldrum, and everything comes to a sudden standstill. We need the doldrums. They train us "to place our trust in God, and not in our own frantic blowing." The doldrums are there to remind us that we are seeking the real God. He is in control, and we are utterly and completely dependent on Him. We need to learn to "wait on him because he is God. He is not in our service. We are in his service." Waiting on God means that we wait until he acts or answers. It teaches us that we are not God.[22]

During these times, we must keep on abiding in Christ. Keep on setting our sails even during the doldrums, even when it seems not to be working. We must keep on practicing so that these spiritual exercises become a habit. And when the wind returns and blows, we will be ready to catch its power and sail the boat of our lives, living every moment with God.

REFLECTION

1. Think back to a time when you were in the spiritual doldrums, or perhaps you are there now. Reflect on the doldrums you have experienced or are experiencing. Why are you in the doldrums? What is God trying to teach you through these? Are you trying to control the wind? Has your ego taken over and you need to let go of control?

ACTION

1. Reflect on your current practice of the spiritual disciplines. Identify one skill or area where you could improve in "setting your sails." Is it praying more, studying the word of God more consistently, worshiping with the community of Christ, practicing fellowship with other believers or something else?

2. Develop an action plan to improve that discipline or skill, and implement it for one week. Evaluate your practice and the impact on your spiritual life after one week. Continue to improve in that area.

After a few weeks, identify another skill or discipline to improve, develop a plan, and implement it.[23]

---

1. This illustration of sailing and setting your sails I borrowed from Wilbourne, *Union*, chapter 11. See also the previous chapter where this illustration was explained.
2. Richard J. Forster, *Celebration of Discipline: The Path to Spirit Growth* (San Francisco: HarperSanFrancisco, 1978), 7 quoted by Wilbourne, Kindle loc 2779.
3. Wilbourne, Kindle loc 2779-2797.
4. Wilbourne, Kindle loc 2779-2797.
5. I review only some of the spiritual disciplines here. There are more. I do not discuss them in depth. There are many great resources out there that discuss the spiritual disciplines in depth. Please read these to learn more. My purpose here is only to highlight the importance of the spiritual disciplines as tools to abide in Christ, as skills to set our sails to sail with Christ in the power of the Holy Spirit. Also, this review is based on and a summary of Wilbourne's discussion of the spiritual discipline in chapter 12 of his book, *Union with Christ*.
6. Wilbourne, Kindle loc 2794.
7. See Wilbourne, Kindle loc 2783-2802.
8. See Wilbourne, Kindle loc 2802-2839.
9. Wilbourne, Kindle loc 2820-2839.
10. Charles E. Moore, ed., *Provocations: Spiritual Writings of Kierkegaard* (Maryknoll, NY: Orbis, 2009), 349, quoted by Wilbourne, Kindle loc 4227-4228.
11. See Wilbourne, Kindle loc 2820-2840.
12. Wilbourne, Kindle loc 2832.
13. See Wilbourne, Kindle loc 2820-2840.
14. See Wilbourne, Kindle loc 2840-2869.
15. Wilbourne, Kindle loc 2870.
16. Wilbourne, Kindle loc 2870-2877.
17. Dietrich Bonhoeffer, *Life Together*, (New York: Harper & Brothers, 1954), 23, quoted by Wilbourne, Kindle loc 2878.
18. Wilbourne, Kindle loc 2880-2886.
19. This illustration borrowed from Wilbourne, Kindle loc 2886-2923.
20. Wilbourne, Kindle loc 2909-2915.
21. See Wilbourne, Kindle loc 2896-2914.
22. Wilbourne, Kindle loc 2896-2915.
23. Again for this chapter I give full credit to Rankin Wilbourne, *Union with Christ: The Way to Know and Enjoy God* (Colorado Springs, CO: David C Cook, 2016), especially ch. 12. This chapter is based on and follow the ideas, thinking, and outline of Wilbourne's book. It also uses his illustrations.

12

CHILDREN OF GOD LIVE RIGHT AND LOVE OTHERS

"Everyone who sins breaks the law; in fact, sin is lawlessness. But you know that he appeared so that he might take away our sins. And in him is no sin. No one who lives in him keeps on sinning. No one who continues to sin has either seen him or known him.

"Dear children, do not let anyone lead you astray. The one who does what is right is righteous, just as he is righteous. The one who does what is sinful is of the devil, because the devil has been sinning from the beginning. The reason the Son of God appeared was to destroy the devil's work. No one who is born of God will continue to sin, because God's seed remains in them; they cannot go on sinning, because they have been born of God. This is how we know who the children of God are and who the children of the devil are: Anyone who does not do what is right is not God's child, nor is anyone who does not love their brother and sister." (1 John 3:4-10)

FINALLY, we come to the passage that raises many questions and could lead to confusion and misunderstandings. Remember, John was writing to the believers to encourage them. They experienced divisions and false teachings. One of these false teachings was that salvation is something spiritual only. You can have a relationship with God but go on living a sinful life. They taught cheap grace, using God's grace as an excuse for sinful behavior. Paul dealt with a similar problem in Romans 6:1-11.

The believers were asking: "How do we know that we are children of God? Who are children of God?"

Are we not experiencing similar problems and questions today?

We see Christians practicing or condoning immoral, sinful practices like racism, sexual immorality, sexual harassment, sexual exploitation, child molestation, abortion, corruption, lies, injustices, economic systems, and practices that make the poor poorer and the rich richer—environmental policies and practices that hinder godly stewardship of God's creation. And the list goes on and on. We see Christian leaders fall because of these practices. We see the double standards of leaders in all sectors of society being exposed. Some of these leaders claim to be Christians.

Christians condone these by either remaining silent or trying to make excuses. It is amazing to see how Christians are making decisions and judgment calls based not on the Bible but on their cultural, political, and personal viewpoints. Some Christians speak out against some of these sinful practices but keep quiet about others because it is inconvenient, uncomfortable, or too close to home. For example: followers of Jesus must be pro-life in all areas. We cannot shout murder when it comes to abortion but ignore other areas where human lives are destroyed, where unjust, unrighteous practices prevent people from being fully human and living with human dignity.

What do we do with Jesus' teaching in Matthew 5:21-22 where he places murder and anger against someone in the same category?

"But I tell you that anyone who is angry with a brother or sister will be subject to judgement. Again, anyone who says to a brother or sister, 'Raca,' is answerable to the court. And anyone who says, 'You fool' will be in danger of the fire of hell."

This should bring us pause. We should stop and think about

how we behave towards others, about what we think and say, and what we post on social media. Jesus also said,

"I tell you that anyone who looks at a woman lustfully has already committed adultery with her in his heart." (Matt. 5:28)

This is radical. Jesus is radical. The kingdom life is radical.

Today, we also need to ask and answer the questions: Who are the children of God? How do we know that we are children of God? How should we live as children of God?

There are no gray areas. Jesus and John are very clear. You are either a child of God or a child of the devil. Children of God live righteously and love others as they love themselves. In these verses we see our union with Christ demonstrated again. When we abide in Christ we cannot sin.

1. WE ARE IN CHRIST, THEREFORE WE CANNOT KEEP ON SINNING

"Everyone who practices sin also practices lawlessness, and sin is lawlessness." (1 John 3:4)

Sin is not living up to God's standards.[1] The law is God's commandments, his will for righteous living. Sin is to disobey God's will. Sinners live as if there are no laws.[2] Lawlessness is an active rebellion against God. Everyone who sins and keeps on sinning rebels against God.[3]

BUT. We know that Jesus appeared so that he might take away sin, and sin is not in him. (1 John 3:5) Jesus is "the Lamb of God, who takes away the sin of the world." (John 1:29) And this is possible because in him there is no sin. He is holy, blameless, pure. (Heb. 7:26) 2 Corinthians 5:21 says, "God made him who had no sin to be sin for us, so that in him we might become the righteousness of God." Peter says, "'He himself bore our sins' in his body on the cross, so that we might die to sins and live for righteousness; 'by his wounds, you have been healed.'" (1 Pet. 2:24)

We have become the righteousness of God, and we now live for righteousness. That is why in the next verse, John says, "No one who lives (abides—ESV) in him keeps on sinning. No one who continues to sin has either seen him or known him." If someone has truly encountered Jesus as Lord and Savior, they would turn away from their sinful lives. You cannot know Jesus, love Jesus, abide in Jesus, and continue to sin.

Interestingly, the Today's English Version translates this verse as, "Everyone who lives in union with Christ does not continue to sin."[4] As we live and abide in Christ, we are free from the power of sin. When we live in the awareness of Christ's presence; when we talk with Jesus and ask him, What Would We Do Jesus (WWWDJ),[5] then we will not sin. How can I sin when I am talking, walking, living, and abiding in the living presence of my Lord?

To remain in Christ is to know him intimately. It is to see him with the eyes of our heart (Eph. 1:17-19), which the Holy Spirit opened. When we know him in this way, we cannot keep on sinning.

However, experience shows that believers do sin. So how do we reconcile these ideals with reality? We will come back to this question when we look at verse nine later in this chapter.

2. Christ is in us, therefore we cannot continue to sin

"The one who practices sin is of the devil, because the devil has been sinning from the beginning." (1 John 3: 8)

The devil has been sinning from before the creation of the world. He led the first lawless rebellion against God.[6] Through his lies and deception of Eve (Gen. 3:4-5), he opened the way for evil, sin, and death to enter into the world. He destroyed our fellowship with God. People become the devil's children by following his example. They continue to sin without repentance.

They continually choose to align their lives and actions with the work of the devil. See again John 8:44: "You belong to your father, the devil, and you want to carry out your father's desires. He was a murderer from the beginning, not holding to the truth, for there is no truth in him."

BUT. The Son of God appeared to destroy the devil's work. (1 John 3:8) Hebrews 2:14-15 states, "Since the children have flesh and blood, he too shared in their humanity so that by his death he might break the power of him who holds the power of death—that is, the devil—and free those who all their lives were held in slavery by their fear of death." This is what Jesus did on the cross and through his resurrection. He undid the devil's work. He freed us from sin and all its awful consequences.[7]

This gives us hope, encouragement, comfort, and confidence. Even in the midst of the most severe suffering, even when we are overwhelmed, we will not give up. We know that God is in control and what is happening in the world is the last attempt of the devil. But the war is already won. Jesus Christ was victorious.

I know it is very hard to have this confidence and hope when you are in the midst of suffering—death, crime, natural disasters, terminal illnesses. At times like these, it seems as if the devil is winning, and it is hard to believe that God is still in control. It is hard to believe that the devil's work has been destroyed because you are experiencing his evil work at the moment.

Yes, Satan is still practicing his evil works. But the effects and the consequences of his work have been undone and rendered ineffective. Even if the devil's work leads to your death, that is not the end. You will be resurrected to live forever in God's glorious presence. That is the victory of Christ.

But what about now? For now, in this moment of pain, suffering, and fear, I cling to the truth that God is in control, no matter what happens. I hold on and trust in the victory of Christ. My Lord is alive!

Christ lives in us. Therefore, we cannot continue to sin.

Christ is without sin. Sin is not from God. So, when God is living in us, we cannot go on sinning.

3. Do God's children sin?

So where does this leave us? Is John saying that God's children do not sin? If so, is he contradicting himself with what he said earlier?

In 1 John 1:8-10 he said, "If we claim to be without sin, we deceive ourselves and the truth is not in us. If we confess our sins, he is faithful and just and will forgive us our sins and purify us from all unrighteousness. If we claim we have not sinned, we make him out to be a liar and his word is not in us."

From experience, we know that believers do sin. And John knows that. That is why in chapters one and two, he told us what to do when we sin. John is not saying that believers are sinless and never make mistakes. He is saying, however, that children of God will not continue to sin. They will not intentionally keep on living a sinful life.

The child of God in us works to gain victory over sin. We stop living a life of sin by being aware of sin. And when we do sin, we confess and repent sincerely. The Father forgives us and the blood of Jesus Christ purifies us from all our sins.

As children of God, we gain victory over sin in the following ways:

- We abide in Christ.
- We seek the power of the Holy Spirit and God's Word.
- We stay away from tempting situations.
- We seek the help of the body of Christ. We find and ask spiritual friends to hold us accountable and to pray for us.[8]

When we are faced with temptations, we immediately take

refuge in Christ. And yet, sometimes, we do fail. We give in to temptations and sin. What happened in those moments? Has the child of God sinned?

No. It is simply the old, sinful self, still living in us according to Romans 7:17-20. This old self came back, bumped the child of God out of the way, pushed Christ from the throne of our life, and took control. At that moment, we were not abiding in Christ. We were trying to live without him. But, the light of Jesus Christ will break through eventually. The child of God in us will confess, repent, and receive forgiveness. We will allow Christ to take control again of our life. We will continue to abide in Christ, and so live the new life, not a life of sin.

If someone claims to be a Christian but continues to live a life of sin (when there is no change, no repentance) then it is valid to ask whether that person has really seen and known the Lord; whether he has sincerely accepted Jesus as Lord and Savior. Such a person must be called to account. Not to judge them, but to bring them to a real encounter with Jesus, so that they will really see and come to know Him. The devil is not fake news; nor is sin. The children of the devil are also not fake news. They are all real, very real.

BUT. If you have really seen and known Jesus the Christ, the Son of God, and have honestly accepted him as Lord and Savior, if you have died to self truthfully, then you have been born of God by the power of the Holy Spirit. You are a child of God. And by the grace of God and the power of the Holy Spirit, you are being perfected to become like Christ.

We are children of God! We are called to live right, practice righteousness, and love others as we love ourselves. And it is possible when we abide in Christ, when we walk in step with the Holy Spirit, when we set our sails to catch the wonderful working power of God's Spirit.

REFLECTION

1. What do you do when you realize that you have disobeyed your Lord and sinned?

ACTION

1. When you realize you have sinned, do not hesitate. Immediately repent, turn back to the Lord, and confess your sins. Next, receive his forgiveness. Pray and thank him for his forgiveness, grace, and love. Then continue to abide in Christ and live by the power of the Holy Spirit.

---

1. See Hortz R. Balz & Gerhard Schneider, *Exegetical Dictionary of the New Testament,* (Edinburgh: T & T Clark,1990), 2, 136.
2. See Johannes P. Louw & Eugene A. Nida, eds., *Greek-English lexicon of the New Testament: based on semantic domains,* 2nd ed. (New York: United Bible Societies, 1996), 1, 757; see also 772-773.
3. See Bruce B. Barton and Grant R. Osborne, *1, 2 & 3 John, Life Application Bible Commentary* (Wheaton, IL: Tyndale House, 1998), 65.
4. American Bible Society, *The Holy Bible: The Good News Translation,* 2nd ed. (New York: American Bible Society, 1992).
5. What Would We Do Jesus? See chapter 8 for the discussion of WWWDJ?
6. See Barton & Osborne, *1,2 & 3 John,* 68.
7. Barton & Osborne, 69.
8. See Barton & Osborne, 70 for these three steps to find victory over sin.

13
BELIEVE AND LOVE WITH CONFIDENCE

"For this is the message you heard from the beginning: We should love one another. Do not be like Cain, who belonged to the evil one and murdered his brother. And why did he murder him? Because his own actions were evil and his brother's were righteous. Do not be surprised, my brothers and sisters, if the world hates you. We know that we have passed from death to life, because we love each other. Anyone who does not love remains in death. Anyone who hates a brother or sister is a murderer, and you know that no murderer has eternal life residing in him.

"This is how we know what love is: Jesus Christ laid down his life for us. And we ought to lay down our lives for our brothers and sisters. If anyone has material possessions and sees a brother or sister in need but has no pity on them, how can the love of God be in that person? Dear children, let us not love with words or speech but with actions and in truth.

"This is how we know that we belong to the truth and how we set our hearts at rest in his presence: If our hearts condemn us, we know that God is greater than our hearts, and he knows everything. Dear friends, if our hearts do not condemn us, we have confidence before God and receive from him anything we ask, because we keep his commands and do what pleases him. And this is his command: to believe in the

name of his Son, Jesus Christ, and to love one another as he commanded us. The one who keeps God's commands lives in him, and he in them. And this is how we know that he lives in us: We know it by the Spirit he gave us." (1 John 3:11-24)

LET'S REVIEW QUICKLY. What is the deeper life? It is living the new life in Christ with love, joy, peace, confidence, and contentment. The deeper life is loving God and others. We live the deeper life by abiding in Christ, and Christ in us. It is living in and living out our intimate union with the Son of God through the power of the Holy Spirit.

In the previous passage, 1 John 3:4-10, we learned that we know that we are children of God when we live right and love others. In 1 John 3:10 he says, "Anyone who does not do what is right is not God's child, nor is anyone who does not love their brother or sister." Love and obedience are the evidence of the new life we have in Jesus Christ. Love is the central test of our faith. Love is what distinguishes God's children. Love and obedience do not make us God's children. Love and obedience flow out of and are the fruit of the new, eternal life in us. We love because we are children of God.

In 1 John 3:11-24 John further develops his discussion of love. Love is life-giving; love is self-sacrificing; love is helping those in need; love is confidence; love is God living in us, and we in God.

1. LOVE IS LIFE-GIVING

"For this is the message you heard from the beginning: We should love one another. Do not be like Cain, who belonged to the evil one and murdered his brother. And why did he murder him? Because his own actions were evil and his brother's were righteous. Do not be surprised, my brothers and sisters, if the world hates you. We know that we have passed from death to life, because we love each other. Anyone who does not love remains in death. Anyone who hates a brother or sister is a

murderer, and you know that no murderer has eternal life residing in him." (1 John 3:11-15)

This message of love is the gospel which Jesus taught and commanded from the beginning. Three times during the Last Supper Jesus repeated this command. (John 13:34; 15:17,17) Love is at the heart of the Sermon on the Mount. He gave us the Great Commandment of love. Not only did Jesus *teach* this message of love, but he *is* the message. He is the visible incarnation of this love. He is love in action. John brings us back to the heart of the message: We should love one another. Love is the distinguishing mark of the Christian life, not an optional feature.[1]

Who are the people God has placed in your life? You are called to love them, no matter how lovable or unlovable they are, regardless of feelings, circumstances, or different viewpoints.

John uses Cain as an example of what love is not and what happens when we do not love. Cain murdered his brother, Abel. He did not merely kill him but did so violently (the Greek word used here means "to slaughter").

Why? Because he was of the evil one, and his deeds were evil. He was a child of the devil, and therefore, his actions, his life, and his offering were not righteous. (Gen. 4:7; Heb. 11:4) Cain's anger and jealousy drove him to murder. People who do not love become life-takers.[2]

Abel's deeds were righteous. Believers' righteous living and their love expose the evil and unrighteous deeds of the world.[3] The darkness does not like the light because light exposes its unrighteousness.[4] Love goes against the world's values, viewpoints, and beliefs. That is why we should not be surprised that the world hates us. When they encounter us, they encounter Jesus. When you truly encounter Jesus, he turns your world upside down. He transforms your life radically. It cannot be otherwise.

Satan and the world do not want that. The world does not like Jesus, does not accept Jesus, and does not acknowledge Him.

They want to remain in their comfort zone. They want to pursue happiness and self-gratification. They hate him because he, who is the Light, exposes their darkness, their evil, their unrighteousness, and their true secret selves. They don't want to deal with that. They want to continue in darkness, but light and darkness cannot co-exist. Therefore, the world hates Jesus and his followers.

The world hates us, because Christ lives in us, and when they encounter us, they encounter Christ. They encounter righteousness. They encounter light, and the light exposes their true selves. Deep down they know that Jesus will expose their wrong, self-centered egos. So, they hate us and they persecute us.

We have passed from death to life because we have new, eternal life in Christ. John 5:24, "Very truly I tell you, whoever hears my word and believes him who sent me has eternal life and will not be judged but has crossed over from death to life."[5] Jesus is Life. Jesus is Love. Therefore, we love others. Love is the evidence of the new life. When Christ is in us, we have God in us, and God is love.

If you don't love, you remain in death and darkness. Lack of love can lead to anger, jealousy, hatred, and even murder. In Matthew 5:21, 22 Jesus equated anger to murder. Here John equates hate to murder. When you do not deal with hurt, bitterness, jealousy, envy, and anger, they are all like a cancer that will eventually destroy you and others. People who do not love become life-takers.[6]

This is serious business. There is no messing about with this. Where is your heart? How is your heart? If there is anger, hurt, bitterness, jealousy or hate in you, deal with it quickly. Pray, repent, confess, forgive, make peace, reconcile, and love that person. Do it quickly before it takes life away from you and the other person.

2. LOVE IS SELF-SACRIFICE

"This is how we know what love is: Jesus Christ laid down his life for us. And we ought to lay down our lives for our brothers and sisters. If anyone has material possessions and sees a brother or sister in need but has no pity on them, how can the love of God be in that person? Dear children, let us not love with words or speech but with actions and in truth." (1 John 3:16-18)

Now John explains the practical implications of this love and what it means. He contrasts Jesus' life-giving love with the life-taking hatred of Cain. Jesus laid down his life for us. The Greek word used here means that Jesus gave his life as a sacrifice, and he did so voluntarily. This was at great personal cost. This is real love in action, an act of the will, not a feeling.

We are called to do the same, to follow Jesus' example and not Cain's example.[7] Love is self-sacrifice. Love is "selfless, sacrificial giving and service. The greatest act of love is giving oneself for others, living for others. How can we lay down our lives? By serving others with no thought of receiving anything in return."[8]

What does it mean for you to lay down your life for others? In your family, in school, in class, on the sports field, in your workplace, in church, in your friendships, in the community? How will you lay down your life for others in the coming week?

3. LOVE IS HELPING OTHERS IN NEED

John gives a practical example of how to lay down our lives for others. James 2:14-17 teaches the same:

What good is it, my brothers and sisters, if someone claims to have faith but has no deeds? Can such faith save them? Suppose a brother or a sister is without clothes and daily food. If one of you says to them, 'Go in peace; keep warm and well fed,' but does nothing about their physical needs, what good is it? In the same way, faith by itself, if it is not accompanied by action, is dead.

We must love in action and in truth. In truth because we must love as Jesus did with unconditional, self-giving love. Jesus is the Truth. His command to love is the truth. His way, his example of love, is the true way to love others.

To love in truth also means that our actions must verify our words. It is easy to speak and say, "I love," but putting your money where your mouth is, that is the test. If you say you love someone, prove it in your actions.

Consider the people God has placed in your life and ask yourself:

- What does active love require me to do for them today?
- How clearly do my actions say that I really love others?
- Am I as generous as I should be with my money, possessions, and time?[9]
- Can I put my cell phone away and give my full, undivided attention to the other person to listen, hear, understand, comfort, encourage, and love him or her?

4. Love is confidence

"This is how we know that we belong to the truth and how we set our hearts at rest in his presence: If our hearts condemn us, we know that God is greater than our hearts, and he knows everything. Dear friends, if our hearts do not condemn us, we have confidence before God and receive from him anything we ask, because we keep his commands and do what pleases him." (1 John 3:19-22)

Love is confidence in the presence of God. Love is how we know that we are children of God and that we are living the new, deeper life.

Do you know that small voice that speaks to you and tells you all kinds of things, accuses you, and makes you feel guilty?

It is called our conscience. Our conscience is our hearts, the small voice that guides us on how to live. When we do something wrong, it reprimands us. However, our hearts are engaged in a serious battle as our old self and our new self struggle for control of our lives.

When our hearts, or conscience, is tuned in to the Holy Spirit we hear his voice, and he guides us to live right. We know when we do wrong because the Spirit admonishes. He convicts us. We feel guilty. Although a negative emotion, guilt is God's way of helping us to avoid sin or to repent from sin and turn back to him. We acknowledge our guilt, confess, repent, and continue to live in God's grace and love.

Sometimes, though, other voices speak through our hearts, accusing us of things, causing us to doubt and struggle with all kinds of questions. Am I really God's child? Am I obeying his commands? Do I love enough? Should I love or do more? Am I okay with God? Will I be able to stand before God in the last judgment? Am I living the new, deeper life with God? Does God hear my prayers?[10] Why am I still struggling with sin in my life? Why do I still have impure thoughts? Why do I have such a hard time loving that unlovable person?

These voices may come from different sources.

They may come from an overactive conscience or an overactive imagination. These cause false or constant guilt in us. Even when we have done nothing wrong we feel guilty. We feel like we can never do enough to win God's approval. Even when we have confessed our sins we continue to feel guilty about them.

These voices may come from the realization that we do not love as we should. But instead of repenting and then looking forward—trusting the Holy Spirit to help us to love—we remain focused on our failure to love. We keep on condemning and chastising ourselves.

These voices may come from Satan's false accusations.[11]

"Your sin is too big, you are such a bad person. There is no way God will forgive you. You are too weak. You are a failure."

Or these voices may come from an unwillingness to forgive ourselves, even though God forgives us.

Whatever the sources, these voices cause us as believers to feel like failures. We feel guilty, ashamed, or like hypocrites. We don't have the confidence to love and live the new life with God. We doubt. We may lose hope and give up.

John writes to assure us that we can have confidence before God. Whether our hearts accuse us or not, we must not trust our fickle feelings. Instead, we must trust God, and remember his Word, his truth, and his promises. He forgives us our sins and purifies us from all unrighteousness. (1 John 1:9) God's love is truly made complete in us. (1 John 2:5) We have the Holy Spirit. (1 John 2:20; 3:24; 4:13) God loves us and we are children of God. (1 John 3:1) The Father sent his Son as an atoning sacrifice for our sins. (1 John 2:2; 4:10) His life, his sacrifice, his blood purifies us from all our sins. (1 John 1:7)

Trust God. He is greater than our guilt and our feelings. He knows everything. He knows our hearts, our true motives. We can hide nothing from him.

When we truly believe in Jesus Christ, when we truly try to love, to obey, and live the new life, then we are okay, because God knows. We can have confidence before God.

When we fail to live the new life, we repent, turn back to God, and receive his forgiveness. Then we continue with confidence before God.

When we love, obey, and live the new life by God's grace and through the power of the Holy Spirit, our conscience is clear. Our hearts do not condemn us. We have confidence before God.

The implication is that either way, we can trust God, we can approach him and be in his presence with confidence. We can come to God in prayer with confidence. We can speak freely, boldly, openly.

But can we really ask anything?

The Bible shows us similar thoughts in many places.[12] This is not a name it and claim it theology as the prosperity gospel teaches. There are qualifications, conditions, and parameters. When we abide in Christ, and Christ in us, we live in an intimate relationship. We have fellowship with God. Therefore, we know God's character, his will, his purposes, and his mission. Consequently, we will be asking things that are according to God's will. We want to obey and do what pleases Him. We want to bear fruit and glorify Him. When we are truly seeking God's will, and want to live the new life, there are some requests we will not make. And if we should make wrong requests, by accident, or intentionally because of selfish desires, God knows what is best for us and will answer accordingly.

5. Love is God living in us

What are God's commands? John summarizes it here. This is the essence of our faith and the new life:

"To believe in the name of his Son, Jesus Christ, and to love one another as he commanded us." (1 John 3:23)

To believe in Jesus' Name is to acknowledge and accept who He is—the Son of God, the Savior, and Lord.

To believe in his Name is to submit to his authority and rule as Lord of the universe and as Lord of our lives.

We submit to him by obeying his command to love one another. This is not just an abstract, theoretical, head belief, but this is believing with our lives. We submit and give over our lives to him. We die to ourselves and live for him and for others. We follow his example. We abide in him and he abides in us. He lives in us and we live in him.

> *"The one who keeps God's commands, lives in him, and he in them. And this is how we know that he lives in us: We know it by the Spirit he gave us."* (1 John 3:24)

Abiding, remaining, living in Christ. This union with Christ is the new, eternal life. The eternal God lives in us, and we know it because he gave us the Holy Spirit. The Holy Spirit empowers us to live this new life, to obey and to love.

Isn't this amazing grace?

All we have to do is believe in Jesus Christ. Trust God. Trust the Holy Spirit. Abide in Christ. Yield to the power of the Holy Spirit through prayer. Pray boldly, with confidence, and God will give you the Holy Spirit. And by the power of the Holy Spirit, you will live and experience the deeper life with love, peace, joy, confidence, and contentment every moment of your life with God.

REFLECTION AND ACTION

1. What does it mean for you to lay down your life for others without physically dying for them? (Although there may be a time when we are called to die physically for others, that is not what we are talking about here.) How will you lay down your life for others in the coming week? Pray about this and identify specific, practical ways in which you can lay down your life for others. List these down. Then go and lay down your life for someone else.

2. What does an active love require me to do for others today? How clearly do my actions say that I really love others? Pray, think about specific, practical actions of love. List them. Then go and do them.

---

1. Bruce B. Barton and Grant R. Osborne, *1, 2 & 3 John*, Life Application Bible Commentary (Wheaton, IL: Tyndale House, 1998), 71.
2. See J. E. McDermond, *1, 2, 3 John*, Believers Church Bible Commentary (Harrisonburg, VA; Waterloo, ON: Herald Press, 2011), 187.
3. See Barton & Osborne, *1, 2 & 3 John*, 72, 73.
4. Barton & Osborne, 72, 73.
5. See also John 3:15–16, 36; 11:25–26; 12:44–50; 10:9–10; 14:6; 20:31.
6. McDermond, *1, 2, 3 John*, 187.

7. John 15:13. See also Phil. 2:1-5.
8. *NIV Life Application Study Bible*, (Grand Rapids, MI: Zondervan, 2011), 2120.
9. *NIV Life Application Study Bible*, 2120.
10. See also McDermond, 191.
11. See Barton & Osborne, 77.
12. See 1 John 3:14; John 11:22; 14:13-14; 15:7,16; 16:23-24; Eph. 3:20; James 1:5-8; Matt. 7:7-11; 18:19-20; 21;22.

14

WE ARE FROM GOD, WE ARE PEOPLE OF TRUTH

"Dear friends, do not believe every spirit, but test the spirits to see whether they are from God, because many false prophets have gone out into the world. This is how you can recognize the Spirit of God: Every spirit that acknowledges that Jesus Christ has come in the flesh is from God, but every spirit that does not acknowledge Jesus is not from God. This is the spirit of the antichrist, which you have heard is coming and even now is already in the world. You, dear children, are from God and have overcome them, because the one who is in you is greater than the one who is in the world. They are from the world and therefore speak from the viewpoint of the world, and the world listens to them. We are from God, and whoever knows God listens to us; but whoever is not from God does not listen to us. This is how we recognize the Spirit of truth and the spirit of falsehood." (1 John 4:1-6)

IN THE PREVIOUS PASSAGE, John told us that we know that God lives in us because the Holy Spirit is in us (1 John 3:24). We are God's children, and we love because the Spirit lives in us. Now John continues to discuss the role of the Holy Spirit in a believer's life. The Holy Spirit is the Spirit of truth, enabling us to test the spirits—to discern and know truth.

How we can remain sane in what seems to be an insane world?

One way is to test the spirits. We are from God. Therefore, we are people of the truth. There are many lies, false teachings, deceptions and twisting of the truth in the world. Fake news is not a new invention. Fake news already happened in the Garden of Eden when Satan, the father of lies, twisted God's words, lied, and deceived Eve. As people of the truth we must not believe every truth claim, every news report, every political statement, every sermon or teaching. We must not believe every spirit but test the spirits, otherwise, we will be "tossed back and forth by the waves, and blown here and there by every wind of teaching and by the cunning and craftiness of people in their deceitful scheming." (Eph. 4:14) Test the spirits so that we can stand against the devil's schemes because the spirit of falsehood is from the antichrist—from the world—and not from God.

1. We are from God

We are from God (1 John 4:4,6) because we believe in the Name of his Son, Jesus Christ. We acknowledge that Jesus is the Christ, that he came in the flesh, that Jesus is fully God and fully human. We believe in the virgin birth of Jesus. We believe that he died on the cross. We believe in the resurrection. We believe that he is coming again. Therefore, we are children of God, born of God, born of the Holy Spirit. (John 3:5-8) Because we believe in Jesus Christ, God lives in us, and we live in God. (1 John 4:15) And we know that He lives in us because he has filled us with the Holy Spirit. We are from God, not from the world.

2. Test the spirits

But we live in this world. We are a people of truth living in a world dealing with fake news, so-called alternative facts, conflicting ideologies, and deceiving spirits. Therefore, we must not believe every spirit, but test the spirits.

Spirits here refer to the spiritual sources of teachings, doctrines, or viewpoints. It is the origin of a belief system. It is what lies at the heart of a worldview. There are only two main spiritual sources.[1] One is the Spirit of God, the Holy Spirit, who is the Spirit of Truth. The other is the spirit of the antichrist, the spirits which are from the world, the world that is broken, under the influence of the evil one—the world that is in rebellion against God. This is the spirit of falsehood.

We must test the spirits to determine whether they are from God. We must test the various worldviews, belief systems, philosophies, teachings, and claims to truth. To test here means to look critically at something, to examine it in detail to see whether it is genuine, to determine whether it is trustworthy and true. Is it coming from the Holy Spirit, from God?

We can test the spirits because we have an anointing from the Holy One. We have the Holy Spirit, the Spirit of truth, who guides us in all the truth. (John 16:13)

- The Spirit teaches us all things and reminds us of everything Jesus taught. (John 14:26)
- The Spirit testifies about and glorifies Jesus. (John 15:26; 16:14)
- The Spirit makes known to us what he received from Jesus. (John 16:14-15)
- And the Spirit of Truth goes out of God the Father. (John 15:26)

Therefore, we know the only true God, and Jesus Christ, whom God the Father has sent, and this is eternal life (John 17:3). God is the absolute source of truth, and we are people of truth.

We can test the spirits because we have the Word of God. 2 Timothy 3:14-17 teaches us:

But as for you, continue in what you have learned and have become convinced of, because you know those from whom you learned it, and how from infancy you have known the Holy Scriptures, which are able to make you wise for salvation through faith in Christ Jesus. All Scripture is God-breathed and is useful for teaching, rebuking, correcting and training in righteousness, so that the servant of God may be thoroughly equipped for every good work.

The Bible is the living and powerful Word of God. It is truth, and we must test every spirit against the Word.

3. False Prophets

Why must we test the Spirits? Because there are many false prophets in the world, then and now. The Bible warns us against false prophets many times. See for example Jeremiah 29:8-9, "Do not let the prophets and diviners among you deceive you." Deuteronomy 13:1-5 warns about prophets and dreamers whose signs and wonders may even take place, and then say:

'Let us follow other gods, which you have not known, and let us serve them,' you shall not listen to the words of that prophet or that dreamer of dreams. For the Lord your God is testing you to know whether you love the Lord your God with all your heart and all your soul. You shall walk after the Lord your God and fear him and keep his commands and obey his voice, and you shall serve him and hold fast to him. (ESV)

Jesus warned us against false prophets. See Matthew 7:15-20 and 24:4-5, "See that no one leads you astray. For many will come in my name, saying, 'I am the Christ, and they will lead many astray.'"[2]

These warnings are still true today. As in those days, today there are many false teachings that sound like truth but are not. We need to test these teachings. What is the spiritual source, the power behind them? The Holy Spirit or something, someone, else? Is it the spirit of falsehood, of the antichrist, the evil one?

4. Who do you say I am?

How will we know whether teachings are from God or from the world? It all turns around a key question, the question Jesus asked his disciples. The same question he is asking us, and the world today.

"Who do you say I am?"

We can call this the Jesus-test. Who do they say Jesus is? The same test applies to us, "Who do we say Jesus is?"

In John's time, people had a hard time believing that Jesus was human. God cannot be or become human. Unthinkable! Today, the world has a hard time believing that Jesus is God or that he even existed. Some claim that Jesus is a mere myth, fiction. Others accept Jesus as a historical figure only—there was no virgin birth and no resurrection from death. He was just a great teacher. Jesus is merely one of the world's many religious leaders, no different than Mohammed or Buddha.

It is not the purpose of this chapter to discuss in detail any contemporary false teachings and to respond to them with biblical truth. We should be aware that there are false teachings, which deny either the deity and/or humanity of Jesus or that teach that Jesus is not historical.

All these spirits are from the world and speak from the viewpoint of the world. They fail the Jesus-test.[3] When you study them carefully, you will see that in one form or another they all deny or disregard Jesus as the Christ, the Son of God, the Savior of the world, the Lord of the universe. They are all focused in some way on the self—salvation by works and trying to save yourself. They do not want to hear the truth. They do not want to deal with the truth of who Jesus Christ is. Under the influence of the evil one, they are opposed to God and God's kingdom in the world. That's why they do not listen to us. They do not listen to the truth.

But what is the truth? Jesus asks, "Who do you say I am?"

We answer and say, "We believe that you are Jesus the Christ, the Son of God, who came into the world in the flesh, fully human, to be the Savior of the world—an atoning sacrifice for our sins. You are the living Lord, who died, was resurrected, and ascended to heaven. You are the Lord of the universe who will return to restore your kingdom."

This is the Jesus Christ we confess and worship.

This the Jesus Christ we remember and proclaim when we celebrate the Lord's Supper and share the good news with others.

5. People of Truth

We are from God and we are the people of truth. Christ lives in us and we in Christ. 2 Corinthians 5:14-17 says:

For Christ's love compels us, because we are convinced that one died for all, and therefore all died. And he died for all, that those who live should no longer live for themselves but for him who died for them and was raised again. So from now on we regard no one from a worldly point of view. Though we once regarded Christ in this way, we do so no longer. Therefore, if anyone is in Christ, the new creation has come: The old has gone, the new is here!

We are a new creation. Our worldview has been changed radically into a biblical worldview. We are now a kingdom people with a kingdom perspective. And at the center of our worldview is Jesus the Lord.

We are not confused or deceived by the spirits of the world, nor are we anxious or worried about the spirits of the world. We have overcome them, because the One who is living in us, Jesus Christ, has already overcome the world, conquered the evil one, and destroyed the works of the devil. (John 16:33; 12:31; Rom. 8:31: 1 John 3:8) The prince of the world has no hold over Jesus Christ. (John 14:30) And the incomparably great power of God, the same power that resurrected Christ from death, is available for us through the Holy Spirit in us. (Eph. 1:19-20)

We are the people of truth, standing by the truth of Jesus Christ. Therefore, we test the spirits.

- We test the spirits by abiding in Christ.
- We test the spirits by being rooted in the Word—studying, applying the truths of the Word in our lives.
- We test the spirits by praying continuously and persistently.
- We resist the spirits by putting on the full armor of God so that we can stand against the devil's schemes.
- We test the spirits by asking, "Who do they say Jesus is?" Do they confess, honor, and worship Jesus Christ? Is this teaching, ideology, claim to truth, idea, proposed action, or propagated lifestyle according to the teachings and commands of the Lord Jesus Christ? If not, then that spirit is not from God, but from the world.

Being the people of truth has implications for how we live as God's children in the world, and how we live the new, deeper life in Christ. We cannot accept, tolerate, or ignore any lies. In today's world, we need discernment and wisdom more than ever before. We need to critically examine everything and test the spirits to discern the truth:

"Nothing is true simply because it is believable, or because it fits our worldview or preference. Nothing is untrue simply because it is unbelievable, or doesn't fit our worldview or preference. As Christians, we believe some things that would qualify as unlikely, or straight up unbelievable. The gospel has changed us. That gospel is 'good news'"[4]

The gospel is truth. But remember, "What we call good news and truth . . . the world calls fake news."[5] If we want the world to believe us, then we must be very careful not to participate in and support the lies of the world. Before you post anything on social media, before you tweet any news or idea, first test the spirits to see if it is truth. If it is not, do not post or tweet it!

"We are people of truth. When people of truth participate in sharing false information, we do not just do injury to the other person and the process, but we also injure our personal reputation and testimony. When we are gullible, we hurt the team of people called believers. In fact, you make the team look silly when you post false information."[6]

Test the spirits to discern the truth. Strive to live out what Paul tells us in Philippians 4:8, "Finally, brothers and sisters, whatever is true, whatever is noble, whatever is right, whatever is pure, whatever is lovely, whatever is admirable—if anything is excellent or praiseworthy—think about such things."

REFLECTION AND ACTION

1. How do you answer Jesus' question, "Who do you say I am?"
2. What have you learned from this chapter? What stood out to you?

ACTION

1. Reflect on and assess your actions, for example, your interactions on social media. Assess how you have been handling truth and what you have considered as truth or falsehood. Are you a "person (a people) of truth?"
2. What do you need to change in your life to practice the truths you have learned in this chapter? What do you need to change to be a person of truth?

---

1. See Bruce B. Barton and Grant R. Osborne, *1, 2 & 3 John*, Life Application Bible Commentary (Wheaton, IL: Tyndale House, 1998), 85.
2. See also verses 11, 23,24 in the same chapter, and also 2 Pet. 2:1; 2 Thess. 2:9-11; Rev. 19:20; 1 John 2:18; 2 John 7-11.
3. See Barton & Osborne, *1, 2 & 3 John*, 87.
4. Ed Stetzer, "Being People of Truth in a World of Fake News," *The Exchange*, (August 7, 2017), accessed December 24, 2018, https://www.christianityto-

day.com/edstetzer/2017/august/being-people-of-truth-in-world-of-fake-news.html.
5. Stetzer, "Being People of Truth," https://www.christianitytoday.com/edstetzer/2017/august/being-people-of-truth-in-world-of-fake-news.html.
6. Stetzer, "Being People of Truth.".

15

GOD IS LOVE, LOVE LIVES IN US

"Dear friends, let us love one another, for love comes from God. Everyone who loves has been born of God and knows God. Whoever does not love does not know God, because God is love. This is how God showed his love among us: He sent his one and only Son into the world that we might live through him. This is love: not that we loved God, but that he loved us and sent his Son as an atoning sacrifice for our sins. Dear friends, since God so loved us, we also ought to love one another. No one has ever seen God; but if we love one another, God lives in us and his love is made complete in us.

"This is how we know that we live in him and he in us: He has given us of his Spirit. And we have seen and testify that the Father has sent his Son to be the Savior of the world. If anyone acknowledges that Jesus is the Son of God, God lives in them and them in God. And so we know and rely on the love God has for us.

"God is love. Whoever lives in love lives in God, and God in them. This is how love is made complete among us so that we will have confidence on the day of judgment: In this world, we are like Jesus. There is no fear in love. But perfect love drives out fear, because fear has to do with punishment. The one who fears is not made perfect in love.

"We love because he first loved us. Whoever claims to love God yet *hates a brother or sister is a liar. For whoever does not love their brother and sister, whom they have seen, cannot love God, whom they have not seen. And he has given us this command: Anyone who loves God must also love their brother and sister." (1 John 4:7-21)*

THIS IS A WELL-KNOWN PASSAGE. Here, John draws together the main themes of his letter.

- God is life.
- God is love.

We are children of God. We know that we are children of God because God lives in us. We know God lives in us because we have the Holy Spirit. We know that we are children of God because we obey the Lord. We love God and others.

At the heart of John's letter is the theme of abiding. This little Greek word that means to abide, reside, live in, is used twenty-four times in this letter, six times in this passage alone, forty times in John's gospel, and three times in second John.[1] God resides, abides, lives in us, and we abide, live in, God. As we abide in Christ, God's love is made perfect in us, and the world comes to know God through us.

1. GOD IS LOVE

Love comes from God. (1 John 4: 7) God is love. (1 John 4: 8,16) God is the source of love.

We do not define what love is. God is the one who gives to us the meaning of love. "This is love: not that we loved God, but that he loved us." (1 John 4: 10) "God so loved us" (verse 11), "the love God has for us." (verse 16) And then verse 19, "We love because he first loved us."

"We do not earn God's love by our acts of love." It is our experience of God's love that causes and motivates us to love.[2]

How have we experienced God's love?

God showed his love for us.

Love is God's action in human history through his Son. Love is God giving himself through his Son.

- "He sent his one and only Son into the world that we might live through him." (I John 4: 9)
- He "sent his Son as an atoning sacrifice for our sins." (1 John 4: 10)
- God "the Father has sent his Son to be the Savior of the world." (1 John 4: 14)

Love is what God has done on our behalf. Love is Jesus, God, becoming human like us, living in the world.

Love is Jesus taking our place and suffering God's judgment and punishment of death for our sins on our behalf.

Love is Jesus being resurrected to give us new, eternal life.

Love is Jesus living in us.

The sending of the Holy Spirit is another act of God's amazing love.

In other religions, the gods demand of people to worship them, serve them, and love them. People have to perform all kinds of actions, rituals, deeds, ceremonies, and offerings to show their love for their gods.

Our God also requires us to worship Him alone, and we do that by loving him and others. He requires of us only two things: believe in the name of his Son Jesus Christ and obey his command to love. And here is the amazing thing—through his extraordinary act of love, through the outpouring of the Holy Spirit, he enables us to believe, obey, and love.

God knew that on our own we would not be able to do this. Therefore, he sends the Holy Spirit who empowers us to believe, obey, and love. What an amazing God! We have a choice, a decision to make: accept this gift of grace and love or reject it.

2. Love Lives in Us!

Yes, Jesus, God lives in us. 1 John 4: 15, "If anyone acknowledges that Jesus is the Son of God, God lives in them and them in God." And God is love, so love lives in us. Love comes from God. "Everyone who loves has been born of God and knows God." (1 John 4: 7)

God lives in us, and his love is made perfect in us. (1 John 4: 12) No one has ever seen God, but when we love, God is seen in us and through us. People encounter God and experience God's love, through us.

Abide, reside, remain, live in—this brings us back again to our union with Christ.

First, God lives in us. This confirms the reality, the truth, the fact of God's act of salvation. God saved us through Jesus Christ. In Jesus Christ, God is living in us. He is Immanuel, God with us.

Second, we live in God. We are a new creation. Our existence, our lives have been transformed, redefined, and given new meaning. We have been born of God. God's image has been restored in us. We live in God by abiding in Christ.

- To abide in Christ is an expression of our loyalty, our allegiance to the Lord.
- To abide is our response to God's act of salvation, his grace, his love.
- To abide is to obey our Lord and to live for him.
- To abide in Christ is to love God and others.
- Love abides in us, and so we are called to love.

And so his love is made perfect in us. Jesus in us, the Holy Spirit in us, God's love in us, trains us, and equips us to love others.

Read again and reflect on 2 Corinthians 5:14-17:

For Christ's love compels us, because we are convinced that one died for all, and therefore all died. And he died for all, that those who live should no longer live for themselves but for him who died for them and was raised again. So from now on, we regard no one from a worldly point of view. Though we once regarded Christ in this way, we do so no longer. Therefore, if anyone is in Christ, the new creation has come: The old has gone, the new is here!

Love is not an ideal we are striving for. Love is an integral part of our relationship with God. Love grows and is made perfect through our relationship with Jesus Christ. As we abide in Him, follow him, live for him, we learn to love on a day-to-day basis. We will have ups and downs. We will sometimes fail to love along the road. But as we remain in Him, as we allow the Holy Spirit to teach us and lead us, his love is being made perfect in us. This is the deeper life, learning to love God more and more, to love others more and more, as we walk with Jesus on a daily basis.

3. Do not fear. Love.

"So we have come to know and believe the love that God has for us." (1 John 4: 16, ESV) We have experienced God's love. 1 John 4: 14 says, "We have seen and testify that the Father has sent the Son to be the Savior of the world."

You and I may not be eyewitnesses like John and the first believers, but we have encountered Jesus in the spirit, in our hearts. The evidence is in our hearts, in our changed lives, in being born again through the Holy Spirit.

Newsboys sing these words in one of their songs, "You're the reason I am free. I'm about Your name, Your life, Your story . . . You are who You say You are. The evidence is in my heart."[3] We have seen Jesus with the eyes of our heart, and therefore, we can also testify that Jesus is the Lord and Savior of the world.

"And the one who lives in love, lives in God, and God lives in him." (1 John 4: 16) Love lives in us. Therefore, we are called to live love, to live in love, and not to live in fear. "By this is love perfected with us, so that we may have confidence for the day of judgment, because as he is so also are we in this world." (verse 17, ESV) Or "In this world, we are like Jesus." (NIV)

We are like Jesus because as Christ is the Son of God, we are now children of God. We are like Jesus because we love others in the same way Christ loved others. (John 13:1,34; 15:9,12) As Jesus abided in God's love, so we are abiding in God's love, and this love is being made perfect in us.

Therefore, we do not have to fear—"there is no fear in love, but perfect love drives out fear" (1 John 4: 18). The Christ we have met in our life as our Savior is the same Christ we will meet in judgment as our Lord.[4] If we have honestly, truthfully, sincerely, and with our whole heart accepted Jesus as Lord and Savior, if we have died to self and taken up our crosses, we have new, eternal life. Do not doubt. Do not fear. And as we try to obey our Lord and love others, we are doing so not because the church is telling us to or because it is the Christian thing to do. No, we do this because the love of Christ that lives in us compels us to love.

We are like Jesus and we are becoming like Jesus in this life. Love is being perfected in us. That is why we can have confidence, now, in this life. That is why we can live the new, eternal life with God, already in this life. And we can live it with confidence! We will have confidence on the day of judgment because, on that day, the work of salvation and sanctification in us will be complete. We will stand before God, perfect in Christ and perfect in love, holy and righteous. We can stand before God with boldness and openness, nothing to hide, and all our sins washed away, white as snow. (Is. 1:18) All because of Jesus' atoning sacrifice. There will be no fear, only unspeakable joy and confidence.

There is also a word of warning here. When you do not believe in the name of Jesus Christ, you have rejected Jesus. If you claim to believe, but do not believe truthfully with your heart, and you continue to live in the sinful ways of this world and for yourself, if you love yourself, not God and others, then you have disregarded and rejected Jesus. Love is not living in you. Christ is not living in you, and love is not made complete in you. On the day of judgment, a terrible fate of eternal death awaits you.

But if we believe in the name of Jesus Christ, confess Jesus as the Son of God, accept him for who he is—the Lord and Savior of the world—then there will be no punishment for us. We will enter eternal life, living forever in the glorious presence of God in the new heavens and earth. We will be living every moment with God. Forever.

Additionally, we can already experience the new life now as God lives in us, as love lives in us, and as we abide in Christ and love God and others. The deeper life, living every moment with God now is a foretaste of what is waiting for us.

Have you experienced moments of extraordinary joy with God when you were overwhelmed with his love and presence? Eternal life will be that experience multiplied a thousand times. No, a million times.

Do not fear. If you still have fears or doubts, then you need to examine your heart. Why is there fear? What is preventing God's love being made perfect in you?

Somewhere perhaps there is still an unconfessed sin. Perhaps there is a selfish desire that you do not want to give up, that you are hiding in a dark corner of your heart. But God knows.

Perhaps you are listening to Satan's false accusations and lies. He is trying to cause you to doubt God's promises, telling you there is no hope so enjoy life now.

Perhaps you are having a hard time believing in God's love.

Perhaps you are having difficulty forgiving yourself for your old life and past sins.

The blood of his Son Jesus Christ purifies us from all unrighteousness, all our sins. Therefore, we can have confidence, boldness, and openness before God. God loved us first. He loved us when we were still sinners. He loved us when we were empty handed, not deserving of love. God has already seen us completely for who and what we are, and he loved us then, he loves us now, and he will love us forever. He is faithful, and his love endures forever.

So, let us follow our Lord and obey his command to love God and our brothers and sisters. (1 John 4: 21) We cannot claim to love God then hate or not love others. These two go hand-in-hand and can under no circumstances be separated.

Loving others includes forgiving others. In the Lord's prayer, we ask the Lord to forgive our sins as we forgive those who have sinned against us. (Matt. 6:12) Our Lord Jesus calls us to forgive others as our Father has forgiven us. "Be merciful, just as your Father is merciful." (Luke 6:36) He is quite clear about this. If we do not forgive, our Father will not forgive us. (Matt. 6:14-15)

Our Lord calls us to love not only our neighbors and our fellow believers but also our enemies and those who persecute us, everyone. He calls us to be perfect as our heavenly Father is perfect. (Matt. 5:43-48; Luke 6:27-36) When God and his love live in us, and we live in him, his love is made perfect in us. And we can live the new life with confidence and joy without fear.

Allow me to quote Newsboys again, singing a song from Hillsong, "I'm no longer a slave to fear, I am a child of God, From my Mother's womb, You have chosen me, Love has called my name, I've been born again into Your family, Your blood flows through my veins, I'm no longer a slave to fear, I am a child of God."[5]

Beloved in Jesus Christ, we are children of God. So let us abide in Christ, and love God with all our heart and with all our soul and with all our mind and with all our strength. Let us love our neighbor as ourselves. (Mark 12:29-31)

REFLECTION AND ACTION

1. What does it mean for you that God's love is being made complete or perfect in you?

2. What are you still fearing? What is preventing you from experiencing God's extraordinary love and living the new life with confidence?

3. What do you need to change in your life to practice the truths you have learned in this chapter? God and God's love lives in us. What do you need to do to live in this awareness?

---

1. See Hortz R. Balz & Gerhard Schneider, *Exegetical Dictionary of the New Testament*, (Edinburgh: T & T Clark,1990), 2, 407.
2. Earl F. Palmer and Lloyd J. Ogilvie, *1, 2 & 3 John / Revelation*, vol. 35, The Preacher's Commentary Series (Nashville, TN: Thomas Nelson Inc, 1982), 64–65.
3. Newsboys, "Hero" on *Love Riot*, released March 4, 2016, Newsboys Inc.
4. Palmer & Ogilvie, *1, 2 & 3 John*, 66.
5. Newsboys, "No Longer Slaves" on *Love Riot*, released March 4, 2016, Newsboys Inc.

16

GOD IS LIFE, GOD GIVES LIFE

"Everyone who believes that Jesus is the Christ is born of God, and everyone who loves the father loves his child as well. This is how we know that we love the children of God: by loving God and carrying out his commands. In fact, this is love for God: to keep his commands. And his commands are not burdensome, for everyone born of God overcomes the world. This is the victory that has overcome the world, even our faith. Who is it that overcomes the world? Only the one who believes that Jesus is the Son of God.

"This is the one who came by water and blood —Jesus Christ. He did not come by water only, but by water and blood. And it is the Spirit who testifies, because the Spirit is the truth. For there are three that testify: the Spirit, the water and the blood; and the three are in agreement. We accept human testimony, but God's testimony is greater because it is the testimony of God, which he has given about his Son. Whoever believes in the Son of God accepts this testimony. Whoever does not believe God has made him out to be a liar, because they have not believed the testimony God has given about his Son. And this is the testimony: God has given us eternal life, and this life is in his Son. Whoever has the Son has life; whoever does not have the Son of God does not have life." (1 John 5:1-12)

WE ARE COMING to the end of this study on the deeper life and falling in love with God. In the next chapter, we will finish with John's first letter. The last chapter concludes the series by bringing what we have learned together.

Perhaps we should do a quick review. What is the deeper life?

The deeper life is to live every moment with God with love, joy, peace, confidence and contentment.

It is growing in our love for God.

It is growing deeper and closer in our relationship with God.

The deeper life is living as God's children.

It is loving God and others.

It is doing his commands, living the Jesus-life that he taught and modeled to us.

How do we live the deeper life?

Our union with Christ makes the deeper life possible. We live this life by abiding in Christ daily, being rooted in the Word, making prayer our first task, walking in step with the Holy Spirit, yielding our lives to the guidance and power of the Spirit.

I like to summarize the deeper life like this:

Know and love Jesus, obey and serve Jesus.

- Know Jesus—We grow in our knowledge of God through Jesus so that we will know him better than we know anything else.
- Love Jesus—We love God with all our heart, mind, strength, and spirit.
- Obey Jesus—We do what he commanded because we love him and delight in him.
- Serve Jesus—We serve him by loving and serving others.

In this passage (5:1-12), John teaches us that God is life, and God gives eternal life to everyone who believes that Jesus is the

Christ. As children of God, we are called to love God and others. We can do this because we have overcome the world through our faith in Jesus. Jesus is the Son of God who has won the victory for us and made eternal life possible. This is the truth! God has given powerful testimony about this truth. So believe in Jesus, and we will have life. Let's unpack John's argument in more detail.

1. Faith, Love, and Obedience Conquer the World

"Everyone who believes that Jesus is the Christ is born of God, and everyone who loves the father loves his child as well. This is how we know that we love the children of God: by loving God and carrying out his commands. In fact, this is love for God: to keep his commands." (1 John 5:1-3a)

To believe is to put your trust and confidence in someone or something. It is to be convinced of the truth of what you believe. It is not enough to say that we believe in Jesus. The question is, what do you believe about Jesus?

To believe in Jesus as the Christ means that we trust him and have faith in him as God's Messiah. It means that we believe that Jesus of Nazareth is God's one and only Son. We believe that he was anointed by God's Holy Spirit to preach the gospel, heal the sick, raise the dead, die on the cross, and rise from the dead to become the Savior of the world and Lord of all.

When we believe we become children of God (John 1:12-13). All believers are brothers and sisters in Christ. We are all part of God's family. A child naturally and normally loves his own father. Because he loves his father, he also loves the father's children.[1] Jesus said in John 8:42, "If God were your Father, you would love me, for I have come here from God. I have not come on my own, God sent me." If we truly love God the Father, we will also love his Son, and his children, our brothers and sisters in Christ. True belief in Jesus must, and will, produce love for God and fellow

Christians. As we have seen before, these two cannot be separated. We are called to accept and love them, no matter where they live, what race or color they are, what languages they speak, what their political viewpoints are, or whether they are rich or poor.

John gave us three tests for true believers.

(1) Believe in the truth of the gospel that Jesus Christ is Lord and Savior. (1 John 2:18–27; 4:1:5:1, 4–5)

(2) Love God and others, living a life of love. (1 John 2:7–11; 3:11–18; 4:7–12; 5:1–3)

(3) Obey God's commands in his Word. (1 John 2:3–6; 2:28–3:10; 5:2–3)[2]

God calls us to believe in the name of his Son, Jesus Christ (1 John 3:23). "Who do you say I am?" Jesus asks. True believers answer with Peter, "You are the Messiah [the Christ], the Son of the Living God." (Matt. 16:16). What is our answer?

Love for our brothers and sisters is the sign and test of our love for God. Our love for God produces love for others. Do we truly, sincerely, really love our brothers and sisters in Christ? Or do we love only special people or some people?

Think about the people we know and encounter every day. See their faces, identify them by name. Now, do we love them as Jesus loves them? Let God's love flow through us to everyone.

Our love for God is shown when we keep his commands. To obey means that we accept his commands, as the principles and the norms for our lives. But we do not just accept them, we actually do them, carry them out, and live according to them:

"And his commands are not burdensome, for everyone born of God overcomes the world. This is the victory that has overcome the world, even our faith. Who is it that overcomes the world? Only the one who believes that Jesus is the Son of God." (1 John 5:3b-5)

When we believed, we were filled with the Holy Spirit, and it is by the power of the Holy Spirit that God enables us to obey his commands. God gives us the desire to do them. It is not easy to obey, but the hard work and self-discipline of following Jesus Christ is not a burden, not oppressive, not an irritation. We delight in doing God's will because we love God. So, we obey gladly. And when we fail, we repent because we feel sorry for disappointing the love of our life, God. That is not a burden, but a joy.

This is because we overcome the world through our faith in Jesus Christ.

Jesus Christ won the victory through his death and resurrection and overcame the world (John 16:33). We share in Jesus' victory by faith. (1 Cor. 15:57; Rom. 8:37) Faith is our power source and our means to victory.[3] By holding fast to our faith, we will not be lured away by all kinds of false teachings. We overcome the world by taking up the shield of faith to resist Satan and the temptations of the world. The world is trying to squeeze us into its own mold, tempting us to conform to the values and principles of this world.

But we, as God's children, overcome the world. That means that we go against the flow. We do not conform to the world. Instead, we do "the will of God in a culture and society, which are bent on doing their own thing."[4]

How do we overcome?

We overcome by understanding and accepting our identity as God's children. We are kingdom people, not of this world.

We overcome by focusing on Christ as our example, the pioneer and perfecter of our faith,[5] by throwing off everything that hinders and the sin that so easily entangles. (Heb. 12:1-2)

The ultimate battle, the war, has already been won in Christ. But in this life and in this world, we must face this battle day by day. Therefore, we must start each day by renewing our faith in Jesus Christ, believing and trusting that Christ lives in us, that we are in the presence of God, that we have fellowship with God, and that we are filled with the Holy Spirit. Every day we must put on the armor of God. We must start each day by committing ourselves to love God and others by the power of the Holy Spirit.

Faith, love, and obedience—living the new life—overcomes the world because Jesus Christ, the Son of God, overcame the world.

Faith—we believe that Jesus is Lord, and the Lord lives in us.

Love—we love others radically by working for what is best for them, even our enemies.

Obedience—we live radical, countercultural, kingdom lifestyles.

And so we overcome the world.

2. Believe God's testimony about his Son

> "This is the one who came by water and blood—Jesus Christ. He did not come by water only, but by water and blood. And it is the Spirit who testifies, because the Spirit is the truth. For there are three that testify: the Spirit, the water and the blood; and the three are in agreement. We accept human testimony, but God's testimony is greater because it is the testimony of God, which he has given about his Son. Whoever believes in the Son of God accepts this testimony. Whoever does not believe God has made him out to be a liar, because they have not believed the testimony God has given about his Son." (1 John 5:6-10)

Who is Jesus? Jesus is the Son of God. But how do we know that? How can we believe that Jesus is the Son of God? There are three testimonies about Jesus.

- The water, that is, Jesus' baptism.
- The blood, Jesus' death.
- And the Holy Spirit.

All three are in agreement and testify that Jesus is the Son of God: truly God and truly human. Therefore, they are reliable, and they meet the requirement of the law for two or three witnesses. (Deut. 19:15 see also Matt. 18:16)[6]

All three are actually God's testimony. God is behind the witness of the three, so that they form a single testimony from God. God the Father himself testified about Jesus.[7]

At Jesus' baptism, the Holy Spirit descended on him, and God declared, "This is my Son, whom I love; with him, I am well pleased." (Matt. 3:16-17) God did that again at the transfiguration of Jesus on the mountain. (Matt. 17:5)

At his crucifixion, Jesus completed the work the Father sent him to do, and at the cross, he was recognized by others as the Son of God. (Mark 15:39)

In his resurrection, Jesus, through the Holy Spirit, was appointed the Son of God in power—Jesus Christ our Lord. (Rom. 1:3-4) The Holy Spirit is the Spirit of truth. Therefore, the testimony of the Spirit can be trusted, and his testimony is backed up by the other two testimonies, the water and the blood.

When Jesus' authority and identity were questioned, he presented five very reliable witnesses.[8]

(1) John the Baptist testified in his favor and to the truth. (John 5:32-35)

(2) His testimony is weightier than that of John, namely his own works that the Father gave him to finish testified that the Father has sent him. (John 5:36)

(3) The Scriptures testify about him. (John 5:39-40)

(4) Moses testified for he wrote about Jesus. (John 5:45-47)

(5) The Father himself testified concerning Jesus. (John 5:31-32, 37)

This is God's testimony about his Son. We accept the witnesses—testimonies of people—in our own legal systems and in our lives. If two or more people give the same testimony about something, we pay attention, and believe it. God's testimony is so much greater and more powerful. God is truth. God is faithful. God is God. He is not fickle and is not swerved by whatever pressures or viewpoints or influences. He is constant. He is stable.

And when we believe, God's testimony is in us. Jesus Christ lives in us through the Holy Spirit. The Spirit of truth fills us, lives in us, teaches and guides us in all truth. The Spirit assures us that we are children of God and that we have eternal life. The Spirit testifies to us every day that Jesus is alive and living in us. And because he lives, we live.

We have this testimony in us. Therefore, we are called to live out, share, and show this testimony about Jesus to the world. We also have this testimony in God's Word. God continues to speak to us through his Word.

If anyone does not believe God's testimony about his Son, then they are, in essence, calling God a liar. When they question, or try to change what God's Word is teaching, when they try to teach that Jesus is someone or something else than what God's testimony, the Spirit, and the Word are telling us he is, then they are saying that God's testimony is not reliable, not truth.

What do our lives say about God? Are we living in such ways that others can see that Jesus is who God says he is? Or are we stumbling blocks, causing others through our example to believe that God's words and ways are not true?

3. We have eternal life in Jesus Christ — Already Now.

Believe God's testimony . . .

"And this is the testimony: God has given us eternal life, and this life is in his Son. Whoever has the Son has life; whoever does not have the Son of God does not have life." (1 John 5:11-12)

God is the ultimate source of life. Jesus Christ is the Son of God. He is God, all things were made through him. He is life, and that life was the light of all humankind. (John 1:1-4) Jesus is the way, the truth, and the life. (John 14:6) God gives us this life through his Son. He sent Jesus into the world to save the world through him. Whoever believes in the Son has eternal life. Whoever does not believe, whoever rejects the Son, will not see life for God's wrath remains on them. (John 3:17, 36)

This life is in his Son, and whoever has the Son has life. This means that when we believe, we enter into a special, living, spiritual relationship with Jesus Christ. This relationship is possible because this Life, Jesus, who was with the Father, appeared and came to us (1 John 1:2). He lived, was crucified, was resurrected, and now he lives in us.

We don't have to wait for eternal life. It is already in us. It began when we believed and were born again. We don't have to work for it, because it is already ours. Jesus, the Life, lives in us. We don't have to worry about eternal life, because God himself, who is life, gave us this life. It is guaranteed because his testimony is true. His testimony is in us. Jesus Christ lives in us. We have eternal life in Jesus Christ—already now!

So let us live that life now—every moment—by abiding in Christ through the power of the Holy Spirit.

REFLECTION AND ACTION

1. How are you doing on the three tests for true believers—faith, love, and obedience? In which of these three areas do you need to grow? Pray about it and ask God to help and show you what you can do to grow in faith, love, obedience, or all three. Talk with someone about this.

2. What does it mean to you that the eternal life we have in Christ begins now, already? How will this change how you view and approach life now?

---

1. John Anderson, *An Exegetical Summary of 1, 2, and 3 John*, 2nd ed. (Dallas, TX: SIL International, 2008), 168.
2. Bruce B. Barton and Grant R. Osborne, *1, 2 & 3 John*, Life Application Bible Commentary (Wheaton, IL: Tyndale House, 1998), 106.
3. Barton & Osborne, *1, 2 & 3 John*, 108.

4. Barton & Osborne, 109.
5. Barton & Osborne, 109.
6. Anderson, *An Exegetical Summary*, 176.
7. See Barton & Osborne, 111.
8. Barton & Osborne, 111.

17
WE KNOW THE TRUE GOD. LIVE WITH CONFIDENCE.

"I write these things to you who believe in the name of the Son of God so that you may know that you have eternal life. This is the confidence we have in approaching God: that if we ask anything according to his will, he hears us. And if we know that he hears us—whatever we ask—we know that we have what we asked of him. If you see any brother or sister commit a sin that does not lead to death, you should pray and God will give them life. I refer to those whose sin does not lead to death. There is a sin that leads to death. I am not saying that you should pray about that. All wrongdoing is sin, and there is sin that does not lead to death. We know that anyone born of God does not continue to sin; the One who was born of God keeps them safe, and the evil one cannot harm them. We know that we are children of God and that the whole world is under the control of the evil one. We know also that the Son of God has come and has given us understanding, so that we may know him who is true. And we are in him who is true by being in his Son Jesus Christ. He is the true God and eternal life. Dear children, keep yourselves from idols." (1 John 5:13-21)

DURING THIS STUDY, we have heard many times that the deeper life is to live the new, eternal life with confidence. We discussed living with confidence, especially in chapters seven and twelve.

We live with confidence because in Jesus Christ we have overcome. We live with confidence because God and God's love live in us.

Here we will explore further what it means to live with confidence and how we can do it. We find one answer here in John's conclusion to his letter. We can live the new life with confidence because we know the true God through his Son Jesus Christ.

We know that Jesus Christ is the true God and that he is eternal life. We know that He lives in us, and we have eternal life. God gave powerful testimony to this truth.[1] Therefore, we believe, we follow Jesus with confidence, and live the new life with confidence.

Imagine you are lost in a dense, dark forest, a forest so dark there is no light at all. I don't know if you have experienced such total darkness, but it is pretty scary. You are disorientated. It is oppressive. It feels as if everything from all sides is pressing in on you. You do not know which way to go, how to get out of this dark forest. It is a dangerous, life-threatening situation. You cannot see anything. You cannot see the dangerous animals which may be creeping up on you. You cannot move. In the darkness, you may fall over a cliff and die. You may trip over stumps and roots or fall into a hole and break a leg. You are desperate. You are scared. You turn this way, give a few hesitant steps, and bump into a tree. You turn that way, shuffle forward carefully and collide with a rock cliff. You are beginning to lose hope. You want to give up.

Then a light appears. It approaches you through the forest, coming closer and closer. When the light reaches you, you see that it is a man with a powerful light. He introduces himself as the Forest Guide, the Light of the Forest. He tells you that he knows the way out of the forest and that he can guide you out of the darkness into the light. All you have to do is take his hand and follow him. You are presented with a choice. Believe him and follow him out of the forest into light and life. Or reject his offer, stay in the forest, become part of the forest, live and die in darkness.

At first, you are doubtful and skeptical. How can anyone know their way out of this forest and this darkness? What evidence is there that this man is who he says he is, and that he does know the way out?

The man takes out his long list of credentials and shows them to you, a list of ID's and licenses that identifies him as the Rescuer of People Lost in the Forest, Maker of the Forest, Keeper of the Forest, Surveyor of Forest Pathways, and so on. Your hope is rekindled. Your confidence and faith grow. Perhaps he is who he says he is. Perhaps he can lead you out of this forest and save you.

Then the man pulls out a detailed map of the forest and shows you that he knows the way out. He shows you that his light has an unlimited power supply and cannot go out. Now you believe. He tells you to take his hand and to not let go no matter what. He tells you to not look around. You may be distracted and stumble; your hand may slip out of his; you may fall or get lost in the darkness again. "Hold on fast, do not let go, and keep your eyes fixed on me," he says.

When he holds out his hand, you take it with confidence. You entrust your life into his hands. He starts walking, and you follow him with confidence knowing he will get you out of this dark forest and bring you into the light, to a safe place.

You step out with confidence. You do everything he tells you to do. You step where he tells you to step. You turn when he tells you to turn. You stop when he tells you to stop. And when your hand slips out of his and you stumble and fall, he is waiting for you with his hand stretched out. You quickly turn back to him and grab his hand. He picks you up. You follow him with increasing confidence because you believe and know that he is who he says he is, that he is trustworthy. He is the true Forest Guide, the true Light of the Forest.

In this same way, we know that Jesus is who he says he is—

God, Creator, Word, Life, Savior, Sanctifier, Healer, Lord and King. Because of these truths, these certainties, we follow Jesus, and live the new life with confidence.

With confidence. Because we know.

1. We know we have eternal life

We know we have eternal life. John says that he wrote "these things" to the churches so that they may know. These things refer to his whole letter and to God's powerful testimony in the previous verses. This testimony is that God gave us eternal life in his Son. Everyone who believes in the name of the Son of God, Jesus Christ, has eternal life, already now. We know this with confidence because we know the true God. 1 John 5: 20 says:

"We know also that the Son of God has come and has given us understanding, so that we may know him who is true. And we are in him who is true by being in his Son Jesus Christ. He is the true God and eternal life."

2. We know the True God

John ends his letter where he began his letter. Jesus, the Word of life, Jesus the eternal life came from the Father so that we can know the Father and have fellowship with him. In this book, we have referred many times to John 14. Let's look at it again. "I am the way and the truth and the life. No one comes to the Father except through me. If you really know me, you will know my Father as well. From now on, you do know him, and have seen him." (John 14:6)

We have seen Jesus. The first disciples have heard him with their ears, seen him with their eyes, looked at him, and touched him with their hands. (1 John 1:1-3) God has given testimony about Jesus through his baptism, his works, his death, his resurrection, the Holy Spirit, and his Word.[2] Through God's testimony, we have seen Jesus. And because we know Jesus, we know the True One, God the Father.

Therefore, we can live this new life with confidence because it is real and true. It is a gift from God.

3. We know God hears our prayers

We can live the deeper life with confidence because we know that God hears our prayers. Jesus opened the way for us to enter freely and boldly into God's presence. We now have fellowship with God all the time, anywhere. We can live every moment with God.

In Jesus "and through faith in him, we may approach God with freedom and confidence." (Eph. 3:12)

"Such confidence we have through Christ before God." (2 Cor. 3:4)

And also, Hebrews 4:16, "Let us then approach God's throne of grace with confidence, so that we may receive mercy and find grace to help us in our time of need."

It is with this confidence that we pray because we know that if we ask anything according to his will, he hears. We have talked about this before in chapter 13. This is not a name-it and claim-it theology. There are qualifications to God answering our prayers —God's will, God's glory, and our obedience. God answers prayers that are according to his will and his kingdom purposes.

Jesus said in John 14:13, "And I will do whatever you ask in my name, so that the Father may be glorified in the Son." When our prayers serve God's glory, he answers them. John said that we receive from him anything we ask, because we keep his commands and do what pleases him. (1 John 3:21-22)

God hears our prayers. We can know that with confidence. But God also knows what is best for us. Sometimes his answer is "Yes," sometimes "No," and sometimes, "Not yet." We also learned that we should pray persistently until God answers. We must pray continuously, without ceasing. And we can do this with confidence because we know God. And also because our Lord Jesus told us to pray and ask in his Name.

In this context, when speaking about eternal life, John tells us to pray for believers when they sin; to pray that God will give them life. God loves people. He wants them to be saved.

When we sin, we repent and confess our sins. God forgives us. And we continue to live the new life. All wrongdoing, all unrighteousness, and all disobedience is sin, and has within it the seed of death. When believers continue in sin without repentance, they are on a path that eventually leads to death. All sin is a serious matter. John tells people to pray so that they will repent, that God will forgive their sins, give them life, and they can continue to live the new life.

But there is a sin to death. The sin leading to death is denying that Jesus is the Christ, the Son of God.[3] Anyone who rejects, disregards, or does not believe in Jesus, is spiritually dead, and will forever be spiritually dead—that is, removed from God's living presence. There are people who reject Jesus from the beginning. They never believed in Jesus. They are lost. They remain in the darkness. They are dead.

Then there are those who believed, became children of God, but then for whatever reason, turned against Jesus, denounced him, and rejected him. This deliberate rejection of the truth is blasphemy against the Holy Spirit because he is the Spirit of Truth. Matthew 12:31-32, Mark 3:29, and Luke 12:10 talk about such people.

Hebrews 6:4-6 states, "It is impossible for those who have once been enlightened, who have tasted the heavenly gift, who have shared in the Holy Spirit, who have tasted the goodness of the word of God and the powers of the coming age and who have fallen away, to be brought back to repentance."

Then there are others who claim to believe in Jesus, but they continue to live a life of sin. They disregard and reject Jesus through their deliberate disobedience. Their intentional disobedience is rebellion against God and indicates that they have never truly accepted Jesus as Lord and Savior or they have turned away from him.

Hebrews 10:26 speaks of these people. "If we deliberately keep on sinning after we have received the knowledge of the truth, no sacrifice for sins is left, but only a fearful expectation of judgment and of raging fire that will consume the enemies of God."

It seems as if John is saying that we should not pray for people who have denied Jesus as the Christ and Son of God. We must keep the context in mind. John does not explicitly forbid such praying. Perhaps John is not advising such prayer because he has doubts that it will have results in this specific case and situation of the churches he was writing to.[4] John's focus here is on believers who sin and that we should pray for them. I believe that we should pray for all believers who sin, believers who have fallen away, and for unbelievers who rejected Jesus.

James 5:15-16 tells us to pray for the sick and for sinners, and he says, "The prayer of a righteous person is powerful and effective." So, we must keep on praying for all, no matter who they are and what they have done. We must keep on praying for them with confidence.

4. We know that we are God's children

We can live the new, deeper life with confidence right now and in this world, because we know that we are God's children. We know that we are born of God, and do not sin, and the One who was born of God—Jesus—protects us; and the evil one cannot touch us. (1 John 5: 18).

Jesus said, "My sheep listen to my voice; I know them, and they follow me. I give them eternal life, and they shall never perish; no one will snatch them out of my hand. My Father, who has given them to me, is greater than all, no one can snatch them out of my Father's hand. I and the Father are one." (John 10:27-30)

Jesus also said, "that I shall lose none of all those the Father has given me, but raise them up at the last day. For my Father's will is that everyone who looks to the Son, and believes in him shall have eternal life, and I will raise them up at the last day." (John 6:39-40).

And John 18:9, "I have not lost one of those you gave me." What more security do we need?

We know that we are from God and we are in God. We know also that the current world is under the power, influence, and control of the evil one. But the evil one has no hold over Jesus. Jesus already won the victory over the evil one on the cross and through his resurrection.

In Jesus, we have victory over the evil one, sin, and the world. We are in the world, but we do not belong to this world. We know the true God. We know we are God's children. We know that we have eternal life.

Therefore, we live this new life with confidence.

With confidence, we love others, even our enemies.

With confidence, we already obey and live the kingdom lifestyle, the Jesus-life, in this world, right now. We don't care if the world laughs at us, because we know the True One.

We persevere during hard times because our confidence is in the true God. We know He is in control.

We do not need to place our confidence in anything else. We do not need any other securities. We do not need other gods or idols. And so, John ends his letter with, "Guard yourselves, keep yourselves from idols."

Now you may say, "Oh, but we don't have idols."

The problem today is that our idols are very subtle, but they are there. They tempt us and lead us away from the one and only true God. Anything that takes priority in our lives before and above God is an idol.

If we complain that we don't have time for God but spend hours before the television, internet, or smartphones, then those screens become our idols.

If our political or personal viewpoints cause us not to love others, to hate or dislike others, to make disrespectful, even murderous comments toward others, then those views are our idols.

If our political or personal viewpoints cause us to speak out selectively about some sins, and keep quiet about other sins, or disobey our Lord, then those views have become our idols.

If greed and lust influence our decisions and shape our lives, then they are our idols.

Family, career, studies, sports, even ministry, all can become idols when they replace God in our lives and prevent us from having fellowship with him. They take us away from God and eventually they prevent us from living the new life that God gave us. These idols cannot save us from or lead us out of the dark forest—the lost world. Actually, through these idols, the evil one wants to keep us captured in the darkness.

We know the one true God, God the Father, God the Son, and God the Holy Spirit.

Jesus is the Guide of the New Life.

Jesus is the Giver of the New Life.

Jesus is the Power of the New Life through the Holy Spirit.

Jesus is the Light that leads us out of the darkness of the forests of this world.

Therefore, we should fix our eyes on him. We should grasp and hold on to his hand. We hold on to his hand through the Word and prayer. We can follow him and live this new life with confidence for the Father's glory.

Reflection

Before you read the final chapter, please reflect on these questions:

1. What have you learned from these teachings on First John? What was meaningful to you?

2. How have you changed? How have you grown in your understanding of God's love and in your relationship with God?

3. What will you do differently because of what you have learned in order to live the deeper life?

4. How will you cultivate your love for God and others?

---

1. See the discussion of this testimony in the previous chapter.
2. See our discussion in chapters 15 and 16.
3. John Anderson, *An Exegetical Summary of 1, 2, and 3 John*, 2nd ed. (Dallas, TX: SIL International, 2008), 189.
4. Anderson, *An Exegetical Summary of 1, 2, and 3 John*, 190.

18

YOU CAN LIVE THE DEEPER LIFE

WE HAVE COME to the end of this exploration of God's extraordinary love. I hope that this was as meaningful for you as it was for me. I pray that your passion for God and for life has been rekindled. I pray that you are committed to set your sails to catch the power of the Holy Spirit, to abide in Christ, and to live every moment with God and for God. I pray that you have learned that it is possible. You can live the deeper life. I want to end this journey by affirming that the deeper life is possible. This last chapter will review the key elements of the deeper life, try to bring all we have learned together, and affirm that we can live the deeper life with confidence by the power of the Holy Spirit.

1. THIS IS THE DEEPER LIFE . . .

The deeper life means to already live now, in this life and in this world, the new, eternal life we have received in Jesus Christ. It is to live with total love, joy, peace, contentment, courage, and confidence as we live this new life every day, every moment with God—all the time, everywhere.

We live this life with *joy* because we know the one, true,

living God. He loves us, and in his amazing grace through his Son, Jesus Christ, gave us new, eternal life. We were born again through the Holy Spirit. We are children of God. This fills our hearts and lives with inexpressible and glorious joy as Peter says in 1 Peter 1:8-9:

"Though you have not seen him, you love him; and even though you do not see him now, you believe in him and are filled with an inexpressible and glorious joy, for you are receiving the end result of your faith, the salvation of your souls."

We live this new life with **contentment** because we are forgiven. We do not have to earn that forgiveness. Jesus did that for us. All we have to do is repent and turn back to God.

We live this new life with **contentment** because we know, believe, and love the true God. We do not love the world or anything in the world. (1 John 2:15) We do not store up, for ourselves, treasures on earth, but in heaven. (Matt. 6:19-20) We are not anxious about anything but we pray to God about everything, in every situation. And the peace of God, which transcends all understanding, guards our hearts and our minds in Christ Jesus. (Phil. 4:6-7)

We are learning to be content in any and every situation, whether well fed or hungry, whether living in plenty or in want. We can do all this through Christ who gives us strength. (Phil. 4:12-13) He is the Creator and Lord of the universe. He is in control. He sustains life. Therefore, we seek first his kingdom and his righteousness, and all that we need will be given to us as well, because our heavenly Father knows what we need. (Matt. 6:32-33) We know the True One, and he lives in us. What more do we need?

We live this new life with **confidence** and **courage** because we have overcome the world and the evil one. (1 John 2:13,14; 5:4) Jesus won the victory. We are strong in the Lord. We put on the armor of God, and we are able to stand against the devil's schemes. (Eph. 6:10-17) As God's children, we do not keep on sinning. God the Father is faithful, His love never fails but endures forever. He keeps his promises. He is Truth. This new, eternal life is true, it is for real. We have it now and for eternity. His Spirit empowers us, enables us to live this new life. So, we live it with confidence and courage.

The deeper life is a God-focused, God-glorifying, Christ-centered, Spirit-filled, Spirit-empowered, Spirit-led life. The deeper life is becoming like Christ, growing fully mature, perfect, in Christ. The deeper life is falling in love with God more and more. And as our love for God grows, so does our love for others—for our brothers and sisters in Christ, for sinners and unbelievers, and for our enemies. All this is made possible by the power of the Holy Spirit in us.

2. Contend for our souls

The deeper life is to contend for our souls. Through faith by grace, we have received this amazing, wonderful gift—the new, eternal life. But what are we doing with this gift? God paid the highest price possible to make this new life possible for us. Do we take this new life seriously? Or do we only see Jesus as a ticket to heaven, an insurance policy against hell? Do we say, "He is my Savior, but not the Lord of my life. Now that I am insured against hell, now I can go on living my old life as before."

No, we are called to live this new life, to contend for our souls. We are called to:

"Work out our salvation with fear and trembling, for it is God who works in us to will and to act in order to fulfill his good purpose. Do everything without grumbling or arguing, so that you may become blameless and pure, 'children of God without fault in a warped and crooked generation.' Then you will shine among them like stars in the sky as you hold firmly to the word of life." (Phil. 2:12-16)

We believe the gospel of extravagant grace, which requires nothing of us. We are called to live out the gospel of radical discipleship, which asks everything of us.[1] We are called to live out our faith, called to action, to obedience.

1 Timothy 4:1-16 tells us to train ourselves to be godly, to devote ourselves, be diligent, and give ourselves wholly. "Watch your life and doctrine closely. Persevere in them, because if you do, you will save both yourself and your hearers."

Contending for our souls is not just about ourselves, but also about contending for the souls of others. Paul told the elders in Acts 20, "Keep watch over yourselves and all the flock."

We live the deeper life through faith and obedience. Those who truly believe, obey, and those who obey, believe.[2] Faith and obedience come together in our union with Christ.[3] When we believe, Jesus comes and lives in us. Joyful obedience grows out of this union, this intimate relationship. The power of the Holy Spirit empowers us to obey. For this to happen, we must make sure that we are in Christ. Remain in Him. Abide in Him.

3. Abide in Christ Daily

We contend for our souls by abiding in Christ daily, putting on the armor of God daily (Eph. 6:10-17), being filled with, and walking in step with the Holy Spirit every moment. (Gal. 5:16-25; Eph. 5:18) On our own, we cannot do it. Apart from Jesus, we can do nothing. We cannot bear fruit unless we remain in Him. Outside of Christ, we are like a branch that has been broken off, it withers and dies. (John 15:4-6) That is why Paul says, "I strenuously contend with all the energy Christ so powerfully works in me." (Col. 1:28). That is why Hebrews 12:1-2 says that we must run this race with our eyes fixed on Jesus. God's incomparable great power is for us. It is the same power that resurrected Jesus from the dead. (Eph. 1:19-20)

How do we abide in Christ? How do we put on the armor of God? How do we keep in step with the Spirit?

By practicing the spiritual disciplines. "Oh no," you may say. "Here we go again! Now he is going to make us feel guilty for not reading our Bibles and not praying enough." If you are practicing the spiritual disciplines daily, good. But if not, well, then you should perhaps feel guilty. This is serious business. The spiritual disciplines are a crucial, essential, perhaps even a life and death matter.

If we do not practice the spiritual disciplines, we cannot abide in Christ, we cannot put on the armor of God, and we cannot live by the power of the Holy Spirit.

If we do not practice the spiritual disciplines, we cannot live the deeper life. We cannot grow in our love for God and others, and we cannot grow in Christlikeness. We should not fool ourselves by thinking we can.

If we do not practice these spiritual disciplines daily, the world gradually takes over our lives. It edges God out of our lives. Remember EGO? Ego takes over by Edging God Out.[4]

We make excuses so easily: "We don't have time. We have our work, our jobs, our careers. We have families to take care of. We have school work to do. We have sports to practice. We have community events to attend to."

All are true, and all are necessary. That is life, and these are part of life. We cannot stop living. We cannot go, sit on a mountain top, read the Bible, pray, and sing worship songs the whole day. That is not what God called us to do. God called us to be good and faithful stewards of creation, our marriages, and our families. We are called to take care of our physical bodies because they are God's temple. We are called to live, work, and govern our societies with justice, honesty, integrity, and love. But we are also called to take care of our souls. If we do not, then all these other parts of life will eventually fall apart.

We spend hours working on our jobs, sometimes working overtime, sometimes to the point of burn out. Thus, we provide for our financial lives.

We spend hours looking out for our families. Thus, we take care of our family lives.

We go to school, college, university. We study hard. Thus, we develop our intellectual lives.

We compete in sports, spending hours in practice, learning

and perfecting skills so that we can be fit and ready for the big games. Thus, we take care of our physical lives.

This is good. This is life. But, what about our souls? What about our spiritual lives?

Remember Jesus' words:

> *"Whoever wants to be my disciple must deny themselves and take up their cross daily and follow me. For whoever wants to save their life will lose it, but whoever loses their life for me will save it. What good is it for someone to gain the whole world, and yet lose or forfeit their very self?" (Luke 9:23-25)*

That is to say, they lose their very soul.

We must seek God's kingdom first. God should have first place, be the first priority in our lives. God should be the focus of our lives. When we abide in Christ daily, when we live out of our union with Christ, everything else will be provided for. We will have the wisdom and strength to deal with everything the world and Satan may throw at us.

Everything may come crashing down around you. You may lose your job, your business. Someone is diagnosed with terminal cancer. A loved one passes away. Something terrible happens. Because you have been abiding in Christ during the good times, you grow and become strong. And when the bad times hit, you are able to persevere. When temptations come, you are able to stand.

When you practice the spiritual disciplines every day, you learn how to sail your life and your soul's boat. Remember Wilbourne's earlier illustration of sailing.[5] The spiritual disciplines are the skills we use to set the sails of our lives so that we can catch the wind, the power of the Holy Spirit. We learn and practice the skills daily. We become confident in them. And when the storm hits, we are prepared. We know how to sail and navigate in the middle of the storm. We know how to abide in Christ and live by the power of the Spirit in the midst of life's storms. If you have never sailed a boat before, or if you have not learned all the necessary skills, you cannot sail in a storm. Your boat will be swamped, and you will sink.

It's good to listen to an audio Bible, sermons, Christian devotions, and Christian music while you drive or do your work. Keep on doing that. But that is not enough, and it cannot replace your own quiet time with God. You are not fully focused on God in these circumstances. We need time alone with God. To be in his presence, fully focused on him. Listening to him, talking to him. We need time to study, meditate on, and memorize his Word. We need solitude, to just be still in his presence. Time to focus on and be aware of the fact that Christ lives in us, and we in him.

These times are crucial for our relationship with God, for growing in our love and knowledge of God. We must make time for this. Whether it is fifteen minutes, half an hour, an hour or two—everyone unto their own. The length of time is not important, it is the quality of the time we spend focused on God, worshipping him, experiencing him, and listening to him. If we do not stop, quiet down, and become silent, we cannot hear his voice.

It is good to go to church every Sunday, and to attend the weekly Bible study or prayer meeting. Keep on doing that. But that is not sufficient to abide in Christ. Champion athletes or master musicians do not practice once a week. They practice every day, for hours. They practice the basic skills over and over. They learn and practice new skills until they master them.

We can live the deeper life only when we sit at the feet of our Master daily—abide in Christ daily, walk in step with the Spirit daily, put on the armor of God daily.

4. A Love Adventure, A Love Revolution, A Love Riot[6]

How do we know that we are living the deeper life? How do we know that our faith is authentic?

We know that we are living the new, eternal life, that we are children of God, when we obey our Lord's commandments. And all his commandments, all his teachings can be summarized in one word—love.

Jesus said,

> "The most important commandment is this: 'Hear, O Israel: The Lord our God, the Lord is one. Love the Lord your God with all your heart and with all your soul and with all your mind and with all your strength.' The second is this: 'Love your neighbor as yourself.' There is no commandment greater than these." (Mark 12:29-31)

Do you see the last sentence?

"There is no commandment greater than these."

This is the deeper life. It is all about love. It is about God's amazing, extraordinary love for us. It is about loving God with our whole beings, and loving others with unconditional, self-giving, self-sacrificing love that seeks the best for the other person, including our enemies. The deeper life is about God's extraordinary love transforming us to love others with extraordinary love.

Read slowly and reflect again, on Paul's words in 1 Corinthians 13:1-8:

> "If I speak in the tongues of men or of angels, but do not have love, I am only a resounding gong or a clanging cymbal. If I have the gift of prophecy and can fathom all mysteries and all knowledge, and if I have a faith that can move mountains, but do not have love, I am nothing. If I give all I possess to the poor and give over my body to hardship that I may boast, but do not have love, I gain nothing. Love is patient, love is

kind. It does not envy, it does not boast, it is not proud. It does not dishonor others, it is not self-seeking, it is not easily angered, it keeps no record of wrongs. Love does not delight in evil but rejoices with the truth. It always protects, always trusts, always hopes, always perseveres. Love never fails."

There is a problem in the Christian life. We mistake Bible knowledge for Bible application,[7] for living the Christian life. We may know and believe with our heads, but until that belief and love have moved from our heads to our hearts, and from our hearts to our hands, until we are doing it, living it, it is not true belief. It is not real, and we are not living the new life.

We should stop making excuses about not loving others. There are no "ifs, ands, or buts" accepted. There are no arguments around this. If we are trying to argue our way out, we need to look deep into our own hearts. It is our selfish ego talking. We should repent and turn back to our Lord and obey him.

We have learned in this study that to love is to give life to someone and to hate or dislike is to take life from someone.[8] To love someone does not mean that you have to agree with their viewpoints when those differ from yours. To love someone does not mean that you condone their sinful behaviors or lifestyle. No, we will speak the truth in love. But we will do so with kindness, gentleness, patience, love, and respect.

Respect begins by putting ourselves in the shoes of others, not agreeing with them but trying to understand them. Respect means treating them with dignity because all human beings are image bearers of God. And when they are believers, the same Christ that is in us, is also in them.

I want to invite you and challenge you to participate in the greatest adventure of all. And that is to live the deeper life, the Jesus-life, the kingdom-life, the life of extraordinary love. Come and join this love adventure.

Just imagine what will happen if we as God's children begin to live out 1 Corinthians 13. If we begin to love all people like this, to practice this extraordinary love in all our relationships, in all our interactions with others, whether face-to-face or on social media?

There will be a revolution, a love revolution. It will be a love riot. I invite you to become love revolutionaries, love rioters. We must become peacemakers. We must not take sides in these culture wars. We must not support or contribute to these divisions and conflicts in our society. They are anti-love, anti-kingdom, and anti-God. This does not mean that we must be silent. No. We must speak out the truth, biblical truths, in love. We must test the spirits, test all claims against the biblical truths. We must be peacemakers. "Blessed are the peacemakers, for they will be called children of God." (Matt. 5:10)

You are a child of God. You are called to be a peacemaker. You are called to begin a love riot. You are called to live a love adventure.

And it does not begin with the neighboring churches in our town. It does not begin with the person sitting next to you. It begins here, with you and me, with every one of us. It begins in our own hearts. It begins with our families. It begins with our church. We must repent for not loving and begin to love. It will not be easy, but it is possible. When we abide in Christ daily, live by the power of the Holy Spirit, live the new, eternal life, then our love for God and others will grow into extraordinary love. We will become love revolutionaries. And it will change our lives and the lives of others. It will change the world. Others will come to know, love, and glorify God.

So, come and join this love adventure! Burn with passion for God. Experience God's extraordinary love, and love others with extraordinary love.

---

1. See our discussion in chapter 6, and also Rankin Wilbourne, *Union with Christ: The Way to Know and Enjoy God* (Colorado Springs, CO: David C Cook, 2016), Ch.3, Kindle loc 654-919.

2. Statement by Dietrich Bonhoeffer. See our discussions in chapters 5 & 6, and also Wilbourne, *Union with Christ*.
3. See the discussion in chapters 5, 6, 9 & 10, and also Wilbourne.
4. See chapter 8.
5. See the discussion in chapters 10 and 11, and also Wilbourne, chapter 11.
6. This phrase and idea is borrowed from the Newsboys song, Love Riot. See Newsboys, "Love Riot" on *Love Riot*, released March 4, 2016, Newsboys Inc.
7. Michael Anthony, *A Call for Courage: Living with Power, Truth, and Love in an Age of Intolerance and Fear*, (Nashville, TN: Thomas Nelson, 2018), 7, 44, Kindle.
8. See our discussion in chapter 13, *Believe and Love with Confidence*, on 1 John 3:11-24.

ACKNOWLEDGMENTS

All thanksgiving, honor, and glory go to God, our Lord. He enabled me to develop and preach this sermon series. By his grace and with his help I was able to turn the series into this book. I pray that this book will enable others to experience God's extraordinary love, fall in love with God, and live every moment with God.

I owe a huge debt of gratitude to the South Umpqua Community Church who took a huge risk in calling me to serve them as pastor; someone with a speech disability and a foreigner. You received Haniki, my wife, and I, with open arms and overwhelming love—extraordinary love. I developed and preached this sermon series while serving this wonderful community. Living life with them, growing together in Christ, and encouraging one another to live the deeper life impacted us, the sermons and this book.

Many authors, theologians, pastors, church leaders, and friends have played important roles in the development of the sermon series and eventually this book. I used many resources like commentaries, Bible dictionaries, Study Bibles, and other books in my study and preparation for the series. Some of these are referenced in the endnotes, and there is a full bibliography at the end.

With so many sources playing a role in the process, I am quite sure that I used ideas and wordings that can be attributed to other authors. I tried my best to reference them, but it is very likely that some slipped through. My apologies where that happened. I give full credit to the authors and sources in the bibliography. Without them, this series and this book would not be possible. This book is not an original creation but uses many sources to develop and communicate this series of teachings on God's extraordinary love as we encounter it in First John.

There are two authors whose books played a major role. Their writings and theology impacted me and helped me to grow in living the deeper life. So much so that I borrowed and used much of their thoughts, ideas, and illustrations. Many times I quoted them directly. Sometimes I adapted their ideas and illustrations, and for a couple of chapters, the chapter outlines were based on their outlines. Even though I reference them in the text, I am compelled to acknowledge them and their writings here. I praise and thank God for these servants of his. They are:

John Ortberg and his book, *Soul Keeping: Caring For the Most Important Part of You*, and

Rankin Wilbourne and his book, *Union with Christ: The Way to Know and Enjoy God*.

Thank you, Jack Painter, friend, and former colleague, who convinced and encouraged me to turn my sermons into a book.

Many thanks and appreciation go to my editors, Rachel McCracken and Jean Pace. Your wise suggestions and appropriate corrections not only improved the book but also taught me many things that will help me in the future. You did an excellent job. Thank you for your patience and guidance. I owe you a great debt of gratitude.

Thank you Haniki, Anri, and Sonja, my wife and daughters, for your love, encouragement, and support. Haniki's comments before and after the sermons helped to refine and improve them.

Anri, for her input and for designing the book cover. Sonja helped with editing and clarifying my thoughts.

I have been blessed to experience extraordinary love, not only God's love, but also the extraordinary love of family and community.

BIBLIOGRAPHY

Akin, Daniel L. *1, 2, 3 John, vol. 38*. The New American. Nashville, TN: Broadman & Holman Publishers, 2001.

American Bible Society. *The Holy Bible: The Good News Translation*. 2nd ed. New York: American Bible Society, 1992.

Anderson, John. *An Exegetical Summary of 1, 2, and 3 John*. 2nd ed. Dallas, TX: SIL International, 2008.

Anthony, Michael. *A Call for Courage: Living with Power, Truth, and Love in an Age of Intolerance and Fear*. Nashville, TN: Thomas Nelson, 2018, Kindle edition.

Ashbrook, R. Thomas. *Mansions of the Heart: Exploring the Seven Stages of Spiritual Growth*. San Francisco, CA: Jossey-Bass, 2009, Kindle edition.

Balz, Hortz R. and Gerhard Schneider, eds. *Exegetical Dictionary of the New Testament*. Edinburgh: T & T Clark, 1990.

Barry, John D. et al., eds. *Faithlife Study Bible*. Bellingham, WA: Lexham Press, 2016.

Barton, Bruce B. and Grant R. Osborne. *1, 2 & 3 John. Life Application Bible Commentary*. Wheaton, IL: Tyndale House, 1998.

Blanchard, Ken, Phil Hodges, Lee Ross, and Avery Willis. *Lead Like Jesus: Beginning the Journey*. Nashville: J. Countryman, 2003.

BIBLIOGRAPHY

Bonhoeffer, Dietrich. *Life Together.* New York: Harper & Brothers, 1954.

Bonhoeffer, Dietrich. *The Cost of Discipleship.* New York: Collier-Macmillan, 1963.

Cabal, Ted, ed. *The Apologetics Study Bible: Understand Why You Believe.* Nashville, TN: Holman Bible Publishers, 2007.

Case, David A. and David W. Holdren. *1-2 Peter, 1-3 John, Jude: A Commentary for Bible Students.* Indianapolis, IN: Wesleyan Publishing House, 2006.

Derickson, Gary W. *First, Second, and Third John.* Edited by H. Wayne House, W. Hall Harris III, and Andrew W. Pitts. Evangelical Exegetical Commentary. Bellingham, WA: Lexham Press, 2012.

Forster, Richard J. *Celebration of Discipline: The Path to Spirit Growth.* San Francisco: HarperSanFrancisco, 1978.

Freedman, David Noel, et al., eds. *The Anchor Yale Bible Dictionary.* New York: Doubleday, 1992.

Kruse, Colin G. *The Letters of John.* The Pillar New Testament Commentary. Grand Rapids, MI; Leicester, England: W.B. Eerdmans Pub.; Apollos, 2000.

Louw, Johannes P. and Eugene A. Nida, eds. *Greek-English Lexicon of the New Testament: Based on Semantic Domains.* 2nd ed. New York: United Bible Societies, 1996.

McDermond, J. E. *1, 2, 3 John.* Believers Church Bible Commentary. Harrisonburg, VA; Waterloo, ON: Herald Press, 2011.

Moon, Gary W. *Apprenticeship with Jesus: Learning to Live Like the Master.* Grand Rapids, MI: Baker Books, 2009.

NIV Life Application Study Bible. Grand Rapids, MI: Zondervan, 2011.

NLT Study Bible. New Living Translation, 2nd ed. Carol Stream: Tyndale House Publishers, Inc., 2008.

Ortberg, John. *Soul Keeping: Caring For the Most Important Part of You.* Grand Rapids, MI: Zondervan, 2014, Kindle edition.

Palmer, Earl F. and Lloyd J. Ogilvie. *1, 2 & 3 John / Revelation, vol. 35*. The Preacher's Commentary Series. Nashville, TN: Thomas Nelson Inc, 1982.

Peterson, Eugene. *The Message: The Bible in Contemporary Language*. Colorado Springs, CO: NavPress, 2005.

Ryken, Leland and Philip Graham Ryker, eds. *The Literary Study Bible: English Standard Version*. Wheaton, IL: Crossway Bibles, 2007.

Stetzer, Ed. "Being People of Truth in a World of Fake News," *The Exchange*, August 7, 2017, accessed December 24, 2018, https://www.christianitytoday.com/edstetzer/2017/august/being-people-of-truth-in-world-of-fake-news.html.

Thompson, Marianne Meye. *1–3 John*. The IVP New Testament Commentary Series. Downers Grove, IL: InterVarsity Press, 1992.

Tozer, A.W. *The Pursuit of God*. Harrisburg, PA: Christian Publications, Inc., 1948, Kindle edition.

Wilbourne, Rankin. *Union with Christ: The Way to Know and Enjoy God*. Colorado Springs, CO: David C Cook, 2016, Kindle edition.

Willard, Dallas. *The Divine Conspiracy: Rediscovering Our Hidden Life in God*. San Francisco: HarperSanFrancisco, 1998.

Willard, Dallas. *The Great Omission: Rediscovering Jesus' Essential Teachings on Discipleship*. San Francisco: HarperOne, 2006.

Witherington, Ben III. *NT221 The Wisdom of John: A Socio-Rhetorical Commentary on Johannine Literature*. Logos Mobile Education. Bellingham, WA: Lexham Press, 2014.

Womack, Morris M. *1, 2 & 3 John*. The College Press NIV Commentary. Joplin, MO: College Press, 1998.

Wright, Tom. *Early Christian Letters for Everyone: James, Peter, John and Judah*. For Everyone Bible Study Guides. London; Louisville, KY: SPCK; Westminster John Knox Press, 2011.

ABOUT THE AUTHOR

Dr. Pieter F. Theron is a South African currently living in Tiller, Oregon where he is the pastor at South Umpqua Community Church. He served as a missionary for twenty-six years in Zambia, the Philippines, and Mongolia. During these years of intercultural ministries, he was involved in theological education, leadership development, and church ministries, serving in various capacities from faculty to interim president. Following his missionary service, Pieter served for one year as a professor of Missiology (Missions) at Simpson University in Redding before coming to Tiller.

Pieter is married to Haniki, and they have two daughters, Anri and Sonja, who live in South Africa. Pieter is a graduate from the North-West University and the University of Pretoria.

www.ingramcontent.com/pod-product-compliance
Lightning Source LLC
Chambersburg PA
CBHW020414080526
44584CB00014B/1316